Surface Decoration

Finishing
Techniques

Surface
Decoration

Ceramic
Arts
Handbook
Series

Edited by Anderson Turner

The American Ceramic Society
600 N. Cleveland Ave., Suite 210
Westerville, Ohio 43082

www.CeramicArtsDaily.org

The American Ceramic Society
600 N. Cleveland Ave., Suite 210
Westerville, Ohio 43082

12 11 10 09 08   5 4 3 2 1

ISBN: 978-1-57498-290-9

Publisher: Charles Spahr, President, Ceramic Publications Company, a wholly owned subsidiary of The American Ceramic Society

Art Book Program Manager: Bill Jones

Series Editor: Anderson Turner

Graphic Design and Production: Melissa Bury, Bury Design, Westerville, Ohio

Cover Images: Detail of "Mandorla," by Chris Gryder; (top right) Teabowl by Eric Serritella; (bottom right) Square box by Anne Fløche

Frontispiece: Fish platter by Ellen Currans

Printed in China

Contents

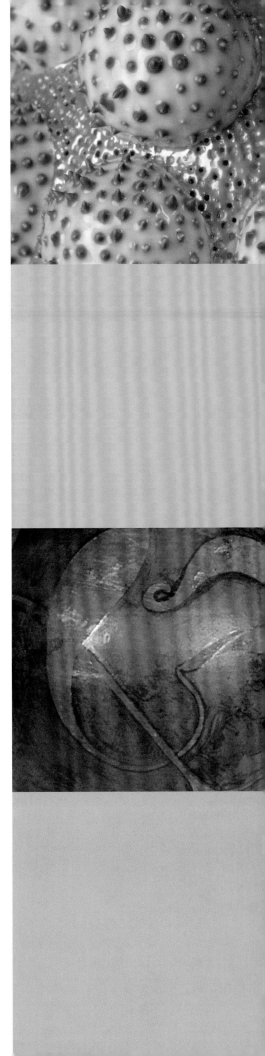

Preface

Everyday I enter the studio, the first thing I pick up is a paint brush. I don't do this to go hit the canvas with oil paint. Rather, I have found that I am much better with a brush than a pencil when I try and sketch out my ideas. This fact has transferred into several water logged sketchbooks and tons of works on paper. However, it is a gift that I have to use the brush, because I am able to see pattern and design before I ever touch clay. I even go so far to add scraps of clay to whatever paint or ink I might be using to give color and texture. So, in a very real sense I am worrying about the final look of the piece I want to work on right out of the gate, not just form. I worry about texture, shadow any number of variables.

Too often, I've met other artists working in clay who fail to consider the surface of their work. They leave it up to the glaze they like or the firing process to make most of the decisions for them. "I love the surprise of opening the kiln . . . leaving it to chance," as they say. The only problem is that they are not leaving things to chance. They have fallen into the most predictable of practices. We know that flame will do certain things, and we can learn how to make glazes and kiln atmosphere effect change to whatever it is we have made. However, that's not leaving things to chance. If you know roughly what should happen, then where is chance? Much if not most work fails at this critical juncture of design and firing, control and proper use of materials. It is a fact that separates a quality glaze and piece of work from a "pretty good form, but I'm not sure...there is something missing."

We who work in clay have all struggled with surface decoration. I don't think it ever gets fully resolved, because if you are trying to express an idea, often you have to step outside of your comfort zone. It would seem that the only thing that changes is the opportunity to keep learning more about our chosen material. In a very real sense, knowledge is power when it comes to surface decoration.

Anderson Turner

Unearthing Beauty
Pushing the Limits of Surface

by Eric Serritella

Stoneware teapot, 9 inches in height. The natural colorants from wood firing complements the surface textures.

Heating clay and stretching it to create texture is a technique used by potters for ages. I was immediately drawn to the technique during an artist residency in Taiwan a few years ago. Since then, I've experimented and developed a body of work I call "Opened Earth," in which I try to show the inner beauty, texture and earthiness of clay.

I prefer to gently influence the outcome and let natural interactions between variables proceed with their course. Beyond reveal-ing the beautiful natural texture of clay, I'm also drawn to the challenge of spontaneous form development. After first heating the surface of the clay, variables such as clay type, level of moisture and wheel speed effect development of the fissures as the clay is stretched. The challenge is to spontaneously make a strong form as the clay is expanded. Unplanned caverns and canyons appear as the piece expands, and these in turn influence the form.

The "opened earth" technique utilizes sand or dried clay for natural

fissures and tools from around the studio for creating patterns. I work with slabs and on the wheel, adding color with glazes, slips and oxides, and using heat on the surface. With many variables involved, this is not an exacting process, but serves as a starting point.

Technique

Center a piece of clay 10–40% larger than you'd typically use for a piece to accommodate a thicker wall (the thicker the wall, the deeper the crev-ice). My walls are usually between ½–1 inch thick. Throw to the desired height using as little water as possi-ble—the drier the better. Straighten and even out the wall with a rib (fig-ure 1). Apply silica sand or dry clay "powder" to the outside (figure 2). While sand and clay are not neces-sary, they help dry the outside and provide contrasting color and tex-ture. Leave clay uncovered at the top for the lid gallery. Tip: Apply sand with clean dry hands.

With the wheel turning very slowly, apply heat to dry the outside (figure 3). I use a hand-held butane torch, although a heat gun or hair dryer works if you have patience. Be sure to dry the surface evenly from top to bottom. The drying time depends on the output of the heat source, size of the piece, moisture level of the clay, wall thickness, distance of the heat to the clay and wheel speed. It's very difficult to quantify the level of dryness needed to get a certain type of fissure with so many variables involved. If the surface is not dry enough, then the clay won't create fissures when expanded. If it's too dry, then the wall will crack all the way through. Once the outside surface starts to become matt and is no longer tacky to the touch, it's time to start expanding the form. Some steam will usually release from the inside of the pot.

Begin to push out the wall and shape the pot (figure 4). This is one of the fun challenges, as it's necessary to create the form one-handed. Touching the outside wall ruins the texture. If you find that the crevices are not starting to open as you expand the form, apply additional heat. It's much easier to further dry a pot than to take make a dry pot evenly moist again.

Finish the top rim with both hands (figure 5) and add a gallery for the lid.

Once the pot is leather hard, trim the bottom, if desired, and add a spout and handle (figure 6). Dry the pot slowly to avoid unwanted

Teapot, 6½ inches in height, fired unglazed to cone 6 in oxidation. The natural canyons reveal the beautiful hidden texture of clay.

cracking of the attachments due to the uneven wall thickness and clay moisture levels. If you're firing pieces with sand on them along with other pots in your kiln, be sure the pieces with sand are on the bottom. Sand pops off during firing and can stick to glazed pieces below or beside them. Vacuum out the kiln after each firing. Sand the fired piece with 200-grit silicon carbide sandpaper. This removes any surface sand that's soft and unstable, and removes that tacky feel of the unglazed clay.

Variations

After throwing your form, score the pot vertically or horizontally with a needle tool or other sharp tool (figure 7). (Note: I've omitted sand on this piece for a softer texture.) Heat the outside (figure 8), then expand the wall and finish the top (figure 9).

One of my favorite texture tools is a stiff wire brush for tight patterns that are great for many firing processes (figure 10). This tool creates shallower crevices and thinner walls. I usually use this tool without added sand.

Another patterning technique is to apply a random flowing design with a combination of shallow surface texture and deep canyons (figure 11). Rib the outside and apply sand, then score with a combing tool or rib as the wheel turns slowly. Change the angle of the tool as you make strokes. A soft, wide stroke creates a combed pattern yielding a series of shallow fissures, while a deep sharp stroke becomes a canyon that opens large and wide (figure 12).

Many different tools, materials and household items can be used to impress patterns on Opened Earth pots (figure 13). I like two discarded wooden blocks I got from a Middle Eastern textile operation. The stretching of

Stoneware teabowl, 3 inches in height, with impressed patterns, wood fired.

the clay exaggerates the pattern they create on the surface. Press the pattern into the wall, supporting from the inside. Tip: If your clay is too wet from centering and opening, use a torch to dry the surface slightly and stiffen up the wall before impressing the pattern. This also helps keep the pattern-making tool from sticking in the clay.

Slab Work

The following example is for a sushi plate or teabowl tray, although heated and stretched slabs can also be manipulated to make bowls, mugs, teapots and other forms.

Pound out a slab 1–3 inches thick, using your hand or a mallet (figure 14). Impress a pattern into the clay (figure 15. Heat the top and sides, but not the underneath or bottom surfaces (figure 16). Don't dry thick slabs as much as wheel-thrown cylinders because some elasticity should be left in the slab for stretching.

Stretch the clay by throwing it down on a solid surface. Throw the slab at an angle instead of straight down (figure 17). This causes the clay to pull and stretch. Rotate the piece to stretch it into the desired shape—in this case, a rectangle (figure 18).

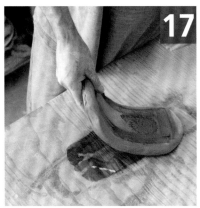

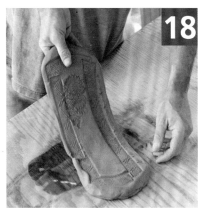

CAUTION

Always work in a well-ventilated area when heating the clay, preferably with an exhaust or fan pulling the heated clay and torch fumes away from you. Also, exercise caution with an open flame. Remember that the tip of the torch will be very hot even after you turn off the flame.

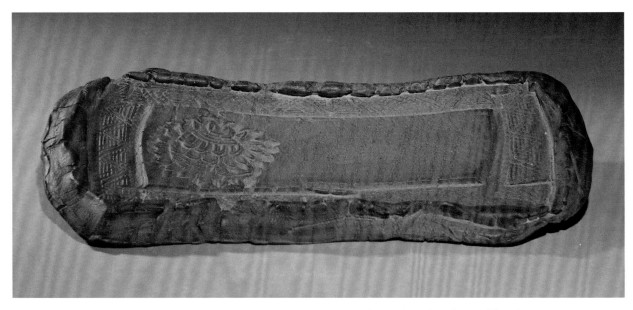

Stoneware tray, 13 inches in length, unglazed and wood fired.

Color and Texture
Creative Bits and Pieces

by Hanna Lore Hombordy

C olor and texture have intrigued me since I first began
working with clay. I wanted
to take advantage of clay's versa-
tility and emphasize some of the
unique characteristics that couldn't
be produced by any other material.
Combining bits and pieces of several kinds of colored clay in a manner reminiscent of impressionistic
painting, and using spots of color in
an abstract pattern, were worth exploring, plus the specks of clay also
provide a subtle texture.

Sources

There are several ways to acquire
bits and pieces of clay. You can collect scraps that accumulate from
previous projects; check for leftovers
and colors others have available;
color your own clay by mixing in oxides or stains; or ask your ceramics
supplier if they offer sample packs
containing several different kinds
of clay formulated for your firing
temperature. Your ceramics supply
house may have a selection of ready-
made coarse or medium-sized grog
available in various colors. They are
also a good source for small amounts

of ilmenite, sili-
ca sand, granular
magnetite, vermiculite
and silicon carbide. I've found that
clays that mature at differing temperatures are amazingly compatible
when combined.

Preparation

It's easiest to begin with small leather-hard scraps. Spread your scraps
out on paper or cloth and break up
the larger chunks (figure 1). As the
pieces get smaller, tap them more
lightly. If the clay is already dry,
wear a mask and place a cloth over
the clay before proceeding to reduce
dust. Another option is to begin with
rolling damp clay into a thin slab.
After this stiffens and is fairly dry,
break it into pieces by going over it
with a rolling pin (figure 2).

With either method, you'll end
up with an assortment of bits and
pieces. Pour your crumbs through a
sieve suspended over a water-filled
container to get rid of powdery residue and absorb the dust (figure 3).

Grog (already-fired crumbs of clay)
also works well. You can work fairly
damp and the assorted colored clay

pieces will not blend together. Make your own ceramic grog by putting ground clay into a bowl and firing it to bisque temperature or higher.

Store your collection in transparent, clearly labeled containers for easy access (figure 4). I've tried many of the ingredients above but have been most satisfied by just using pieces of actual clay or grog incorporated into my work.

Testing

Fire a few test samples using different clay combinations. This helps you figure out how to best distribute your bits and pieces, and helps you decide what size you'd like them to be. Sprinkle your selections onto

damp slabs of clay and press them in with a rolling pin or paddle (figure 5). Put a clear glaze on part of your tests to see if you prefer the glazed look. Identify all the materials used on the back of the sample tests (figure 6).

Picking up the pieces

While you could merely sprinkle the clay crumbs on the surface of a damp vessel, you'll discover that a majority will fall off while drying or after firing. My favorite method for encouraging pieces to stick is to work with a closed form. I throw a cylinder, round it out and gently shape the top inward until the sides join together in the center (figure 7). This traps air inside the vessel and

provides a firm working surface. The clay is too soft to handle immediately after throwing, so wait a while, then wheel trim the bottom as far as possible. Next, cut the piece off the bat and set it aside to firm up (figure 8). Use a rib for further hand trimming on the bottom, although the form doesn't need to be perfectly smooth.

When your form is firm enough to withstand handling, but not so stiff that it cannot change shape, place on a smooth flat surface (figure 9). Pad with a few sheets of newspaper and cover with a soft cloth. Rolling evens out the shape and prevents unwanted marks. Uneven rolling alters the shape of a vessel while even rolling in all directions results in an almost perfectly spherical shape.

Once you've attained the shape you want, randomly sprinkle pieces on the dry cloth. Roll the piece over the clay bits to help press them into the vessel (figure 10). The clay should be soft enough so that most of the crumbs stick. To further imbed the clay crumbs into the vessel, use a paddle with a gentle rhythmic touch, aiming in a different direction with each stroke and causing as little stress as possible on the form (figure 11). Persistent gentle paddling results in maintaining a smooth and elegant shape. At this point, you should be aware of two possible problems: First, paddling may cause the form to become too

You may treat the clay with a bit of reckless abandon, revealing all the marks of the paddle and the construction process (figure 12), but don't overdo it!

Finishing

If working with an enclosed shape, set it aside for a while but be careful not to let it shrink and get too dry. There's air trapped inside that can't shrink so you must help it escape with a needle prick. You can finish the piece by cutting a hole into the form with a hole cutter or fettling knife. Tip: When using a knife, make a straight cut, then cut out the circle. This way, should part or all of the cutout fall into the form, it will be in two smaller sections (figure 13). Add a thrown or handbuilt spout, rim or neck (figure 14).

dry to accept additional crumbs and the surface may begin to crack. If this happens, evenly spray the form with a small amount of water. Wait a while for this to sink in because the moisture needs to penetrate gradually. Don't keep adding water or you'll get puddles on your surface, and the several colors of clay will soften and fuse. Should this happen, you can still save the work later by letting it dry totally and giving it a very light sanding. Second, make sure your paddle doesn't become dirty. Wipe off traces of clay with a damp cloth and let the paddle dry before you proceed.

There are invariably some little indentations or craters in the surface where a few bits and pieces have fallen off. These are not objectionable from a design standpoint for they are little shadowy spots that add to the texture. They are negative spaces that contrast with the positive areas provided by the bits and pieces, and firing this work should not present a problem. Bisque and glaze fire as you normally would for the clay you are using. Occasionally, I spray a light coating of clear glaze over the outside of a piece, but I really prefer the unglazed look. If your work is sculptural and without glaze, single firing is appropriate.

Ellen Currans
Textured Slabs

by Ginger Steele

One day in 1960, an unexpected delivery truck pulled up to Ellen and Tom Currans' home in southern California. It carried a one-speed potter's wheel built from a square, green Maytag washing machine, sent by her brother who had just begun his career as an industrial arts teacher. Ellen had started taking night-school ceramics classes at Pasadena City College in 1957. With three small children under four, the gift of a wheel made it possible for her to work at home. It was soon joined by an 8-cubic-foot updraft kiln rescued from its previous duty of firing garden gnomes.

Ellen grew up in the Okanogan Valley of north central Washington, and she and Tom met and married at the University of Washington in Seattle. For three years Ellen studied clothing, textiles and art, unaware of the ceramics studio on campus. She was deeply impressed by and attracted to the new Scandinavian designs that were finding their way into home furnishings, and the simple, clean lines of Northwest home architecture. Texture, natural materials, and functionality were at the heart of the new aesthetic, and this has been a major influence on her pottery.

In 1965 the Currans family moved back to the Northwest. Before they

"Fish Platter,"
21 inches in length,
slab-built stoneware, with verdigris
glaze, and fired to
cone 10.

Tray, 12 inches in length, mug, and small creamer and sugar holder, thrown and slab-built stoneware, with soft blue matt glaze, fired to cone 10.

left, they held a yard sale and Ellen sold her first pots to the neighbors. She describes them as "thin-lipped, fat-bottomed, with scraggley glazes." In Oregon, they purchased a farm near Dundee, southwest of Portland, where they still live. Their first home on the property was a farmhouse built in 1895. The wheel occupied a place in the kitchen and pots were dried in the dining room. When company came, a piece of oilcloth covered the wheel. Soon, Tom had a small cottage moved nearer to the house, connected it with a porch, and Ellen had her first real studio. They called it Cedar Pond Pottery.

Feeling a need for more training, Ellen began attending classes at Portland State in 1967, and continued for five quarters. Not finding what she wanted in the classwork,

Ellen decided to just start working at home, and began to collect ceramic books and journals, take workshops, and in 1970, spent a month traveling in Japan with Carlton Ball and 25 other potters.

Ten years after moving to Oregon, Tom left his position as a mechanical engineer at Tektronix to build a new passive solar home on their property. Selling twenty acres and the old farmhouse, they and three teenage kids moved into a 50-foot trailer for the duration of the construction. A studio was built and work on the house was begun but Ellen's growing pottery business called for more and more of Tom's time.

Tom mixes and pugs clay, keeps the large glaze buckets filled, loads and unloads the bisque kiln, and unloads and sands the glazed pots. He

Square cookie plate, 7 inches square, handled baking dish, and small pourer, thrown and slab-built stoneware with Oribe glaze, fired to cone 10, by Ellen Currans.

built the studio and all its additions, maintains and adapts equipment, hauls clay and glaze materials, and shares all the work of setting up and working shows. His technical training and physical strength have been a perfect foil for her creative work.

Ellen's studio is uniquely orderly, clean and welcoming. In the main room the walls are lined with books, periodicals, and Ellens' notebooks from over 45 years of thinking about and working with clay. Other tall shelves are filled with tools and pat-

terns and slowly drying new work. There's a woodstove, a bed for Shino the pug and a small efficient kitchen that used to double as glazing space. Behind a central desk and wall of books is a tidy area with two wheels, and an adjacent space with a motorized slab roller. It's here that Ellen forms her most individual work. The slab roller is surrounded by every imaginable object that a potter might use to make a mark on clay, as well as numerous items used as molds for her textured slab work. Most of

Textured Slabs

The stoneware Tom brings from the pugmill for slabs is stiffer than for throwing, and Ellen whacks the pug down with a mallet in preparation for rolling. The clay is encased in canvas and the motor drones as it presses the clay into a flat, firm slab. Ellen smoothes the surface with a window squeegee and brushes the suce with cornstarch. She then carefully places a precut piece of textured paper on the slab. This will define the area that will be the center of the tray or platter. The slab is passed again through the slab roller, registering the design on the surface of the clay. For some forms a rubber stamp or stencil adds complexity.

A mold form which fits the proportions of the textured design, has been brushed with WD-40 to keep the clay from sticking to the form and to allow her to gently move the slab until the design is precisely located in the form. Laying a thin plastic film over the clay, she works the slab into the form using a *pounce* (a cup or so of fine grog held by a rubber band in a small square of tightly woven sheeting). This allows her to press the clay gently into the mold without distorting the freshly textured surface. She meticulously bevels the rim of the piece at the edge of the form to ensure that the clay releases as it dries and shrinks.

Currans finishes some pieces with thrown rims and handles, and keeps all works under plastic film for several days before drying them very slowly in a damp cupboard. After bisque firing, she applies glazes that will accentuate the texture by breaking over edges and pooling slightly in low spots.

In her Cedar Pond Pottery studio, Ellen Currans adds a woodblock design to the center of a freshly textured slab.

these forms are recycled from local thrift and antique stores. There are glass, wood and plastic trays and low bowls of every shape and size, and hundreds of textured paper patterns that Ellen uses to impart imagery to clay. A separate room for mixing glazes and glazing, storing bisque, and loading the kiln was enclosed in 2003 when they rebuilt and moved their MFT car kiln to an all-metal kiln shed. In the mid '80s, a 12×14-foot showroom was built onto the front of the studio.

Ellen decided in the 1980s that selling to galleries or wholesaling was not the way she wanted to market her work. From the beginning she has chosen to keep her prices reasonable enough that people use her work for their everyday dishes and buy more as time goes on. The pots and platters make sense in the lives of the people who use them. They impart dignity and beauty to the presentation of food and to the daily domestic rituals that are the substance of our lives. Ellen's own love of cooking and serving food, and her deeply hospitable nature, have been as much a part of the formation of the aesthetic of her work as have been any ceramics class she has attended. Ellen's work is also unique in that it is at ease in many surroundings; it is contemporary in form and decoration, as well as complementary to the Craftsman tradition that is a part of many Pacific Northwest homes.

David Gamble
Texture from Sewer Covers

by Paul Andrew Wandless

Sewer Cover Wall Relief Tiles. Explore different textures and images around your home or studio to find hidden compositions. The construction process of the wall relief is the same regardless of what image you have in mind.

Artists often look for hidden compositions existing in the mundane, ordinary and commonplace objects of everyday life. It's easy to appreciate and enjoy the vibrant color of flowers, the way light sparkles on ripples in the ocean or the beauty of a summer sunset. More challenging, though, is enjoying the fascinating designs and images surrounding us in the simple form of textured surfaces. Manhole covers and storm drain grates are everyday items not immediately thought of as aesthetically pleasing surfaces. These so-called ordinary surfaces typically go unnoticed and

start to become invisible unless, of course, we are trying to avoid or step around them. Fortunately, the hidden compositions and patterns in these quiet iron circles are noticed and transformed into works of art by David Gamble of Indianapolis, Indiana.

Looking Down

When David looks at manhole covers and grates, he sees pattern, line and low-relief opportunities for terracotta wall pieces. He enjoys capturing the interesting shapes, textures, images and text of manhole covers in a clay relief. He's not just trying to document or get a record of the

manhole; he's looking for an interesting composition or combination of elements already existing on its surface. Most relief prints are just small specific sections of the manhole cover and the original source of the relief is not obvious.

The process of lifting/pulling a relief from a textured surface is an image transfer technique. It's very similar to making a charcoal rubbing except you substitute clay for paper. Printmaking techniques and ceramics have been combined throughout history, and exciting work has been created pairing these two media.

David uses Amaco's terra-cotta clay no. 77, a heavily grogged clay. The grog opens up the clay body and promotes even drying, which keeps his wall pieces flat during the drying and firing process. He also enjoys the rich, dark-red color of the terra

cotta after it is fired to cone 03, and the contrast it provides for his gold luster glazes.

Process

David starts by rolling slabs that are about ½ inch thick. This allows him to get a deeper impression and still maintain an adequate thickness in the recessed areas to prevent cracking. If the slab is too thin, it merely conforms to the surface and doesn't actually receive an impression. If you use canvas while rolling the slab, smooth the surface with a soft rib so it is clean, clear and ready to receive the image (figure 1). Roll out a few extra slabs for test prints and for constructing walls later in the process.

Place the canvas-backed clay slab on a large wooden board and carry it to a manhole or storm-drain cover. Take a brush in case any debris

needs to be removed from the cover or grate. Stand the board on edge and position in front of the area of interest (figure 2), flop the slab down onto the grate, and rub with mild pressure to create a deeper relief (figure 3). Extra pressure works especially well when pulling a complex texture from the asphalt surrounding a grate.

Gently but quickly pull the slab from the grate (figure 4) and lay it back onto the board (figure 5). Take a look at the image you just pulled to see if it has the detail and depth that you need for your wall piece. As is the case with most new endeavors, your first transfer may not meet your expectations. Make a test print or two to practice how much pressure is needed for the relief, and how best to line up your slab to get the section you desire.

Since David's manhole reliefs are part of an ongoing series, he has a board precut to specific dimensions so they are consistent. Place the board over the relief and crop the areas of interest to determine the orientation (figure 6). Besides pulling the print, this is the most important step of the process. Careful consideration goes into determining the compositional balance of shape, form, line and space.

It's important to figure out in advance how you will install or hang the piece to ensure your work can be hung easily and securely. For hanging brackets, David attaches small slabs of clay with holes punched through them. To do this, turn the trimmed relief over and score the perimeter with a wire tool (figure 7). Cut eight square coils from the remaining ½-inch slab, then score and spray them with apple cider vinegar (figure 8). (Note: Instead of joining slip, David sprays straight apple cider vinegar over the scored areas. Build the walls two coils high around the perimeter, and firmly press and smooth them during the construction process.

After determining which end is the top, cut, score and spray two clay gussets to be used as hanging brackets. The gussets should be placed approximately a third of the way down from the top and trimmed to match the height of the walls (figure 9). For added strength and structural integrity, press and smooth a coil into all the interior seams (figure 10). Poke holes with a pointed tool through the center of the hanging brackets (figure 11) for heavy gauge wire to be strung through when ready to hang.

David finishes with stamping the date and number of the print on the back, and signs his name. The wall piece needs to stiffen to leather hard before it's turned over to avoid sagging. Once flipped, smooth the corners by hand to remove the sharp edges (figure 12). The rounded corners also help the surfaces dry more evenly and avoid unnecessary cracking or separating.

Finishing touches

David bisque fires to cone 03, then brushes on a black copper oxide wash into the recessed areas of the relief for added visual depth. After the wash has dried, he applies three coats of Amaco L-518 Lustre Gold, allowing the glaze to dry thoroughly between coats. After the glaze firing to cone 03, a 10- or 12-gauge solid copper wire is strung through the holes in the brackets and the piece is ready to hang.

Rolling Stamps

by William Shinn

Rolling stamps give you a practical way to create repeating designs. Combining stamps provides even more design opportunities.

The early Greek potters used small rolls of clay that had been carved on the surfaces to produce repeated patterns on their freshly thrown forms. However, little more has been done with this technique by subsequent potters. This is understandable, since larger rolling stamps would, of course, distort a freshly thrown piece. With the increased interest in handbuilt, press-molded and extruded forms, the possibilities for texturing flat surfaces with rolling stamps on a larger scale can be more thoroughly explored.

The simplest method of creating rolling stamps is to roll a clay slab around a tubular shape, such as a cardboard tube, wooden dowel or plastic pipe. These produce a rigid backing when applying a texture to the slabs. A piece of newspaper placed between the form and the clay will prevent sticking when removing the support. Removal should be performed as soon as possible before any shrinkage takes place.

Process

Stamps also can be made by throwing a cylindrical or conical form (figure 1). The thrown stamps are created like miniature steamer casseroles. The center spout is pulled up and compressed to an opening the size of the dowel (with allowance for shrinkage). The outer wall is then raised to form the working surface of the stamp, which will be carved at the proper stage of drying. Make sure that the outer surface is perpendicular to the wheel head (figure 2).

The use of an extruder can also produce tubular shapes for rolling stamps. The ends can be filled in, leaving small holes in the center to

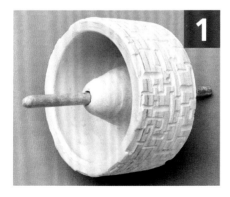

allow dowels to be used as handles. Bisqued clay produces an ideal stamp with its combination of porosity, strength and permanence. Make the walls as thick as possible because a thin wall can't withstand the heavy pressure and becomes quickly saturated, losing its resistance to sticking. Use a hair dryer to solve this problem.

After creating and firing the stamps, their use is quite simple. The cylinders are rolled over the surface of the clay with the palm of the hand while varying the pressure to correspond to the width of the stamp. For small stamps, I prefer throwing the forms and using them

with dowels for handles—much like rolling pins. They are more easily guided in a straight or curved line than the wider and heavier cylindrical stamps.

The rolling stamp is ideal for quickly decorating a platter rim. The stamp, held rigidly in a fixed position, quickly prints out the repeated pattern as the wheel spins. Lifting at the right moment can be tricky. A little practice is recommended when starting this project (figure 3).

Besides carving, the surface pattern can be created a variety of ways—utilizing simple stamps (repeated or varied), rolling the clay over natural or manmade surfaces,

stretching the clay pattern while flat before wrapping around a cylinder, etc. The possibilities are endless. You also may notice that the impressed negative design on the clay can be quite different from the positive design of the stamp.

Very effective surfaces can be obtained by cutting the cylinders into sections and reassembling the parts into different positions. This can be done when the stamps are leather hard and then glued back together after bisque firing. Such a rolling stamp can produce a variety of results (figure 4 and 5). Other tools can add further interest to the surface (figure 6).

For producing an overall surface, or for creating unconventionally shaped tiles, design a cylinder with matched outer edges. This creates a repeated pattern that fits within itself and create a continuous surface when rolled side by side (figure 7).

A conical thrown form can be used to produce a round design (figure 8). The conical stamp can be combined with the handled stamp to increase the complexity of the design.

Unlike a thrown form, an extruded shape possessing flat surfaces is an excellent form for stamping when supported from the inside. Newspaper or cloth can be used to prevent sticking (figure 9).

Simply wrapping clay around a wooden or cardboard shape presents an ideal backing for applying a stamp design. The imprinted design has an advantage over a raised pattern because you can gently rotate the work face down for support with little distortion of the design. An attached handle inside the mold helps facilitate its removal (figure 10).

When glazing the work, the imprinted design is ideal for inlaying color. After applying the first glaze, the surface is brushed off, resulting in a neatly inlaid color. Another contrasting glaze can be added over the entire surface. You can also stain the textured areas and glaze other sections of the pot. The possible variations in glazing are as numerous as the variations in stamping the ware.

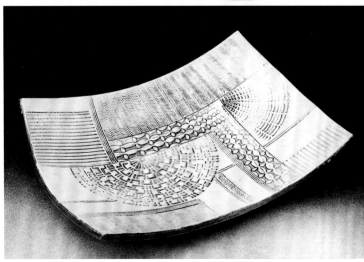

Clockwise from top left:

Saddle form, 18 inches in height, slab built using conical and rolling stamps.

Rectangular platter, 21 inches in width, slab built using a combination of conical and rolling stamps.

Vase, 19 inches in height, slab built using a stamp with matched outer edges.

Sprigs from Nature

by Judi Munn

Sprig molds provide a great way to decorate your work. Made from fossils, shells, found objects, or by carving into clay, there's no limit to the variety.

When we first started firing with wood, I got really interested in texture. One of the things that I began to experiment with was creating press molds of shells that could be used to add sprigs. I had a lifetime shell collection from around the world, and I was glad to finally have a reason to use them.

Sprigs are press-molded clay pieces added to leather-hard work. They are created using small molds made of bisque-fired clay or plaster. Wedgwood Jasperware from England is a well-known example of sprig-decorated ware. While Wedgwood's patterns are very intricate, simple sprig molds can be made using almost any object or hand-modeled relief that does not have undercuts.

I use seashells as a motif even though we live in the land-locked Ozarks. On the surface, this might seem a bit out of place, but a trip to any Ozark stream proves otherwise. The creek beds are littered with fossils such as crinoids, sea fan and brachiopods. So, it's natural that I use fossils, as well as the seashells. I'm particularly fond of the beautifully spiraled ammonites.

Historically, sprigs were removed from the mold then applied to the pot. You can also press the sprig onto the pot while it is still in the mold, which can either be a gentle press or a deep one that changes the contour of the pot. Doing this requires an interesting shape for the whole sprig mold.

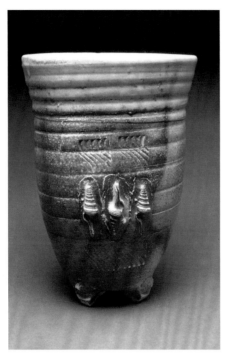 

Sprigs can be used in several ways. They've been used as feet and in a surface decoration on the 7-inch vase (top left). On the bottle (top right), sprigs form the handles and glazing highlights a sprig decoration on the side. With the punch bowl (bottom), sprigs are used in a repeat pattern around the shoulder of the form. All pieces shown here have been fired to cone 9 in a wood-fired kiln.

Process

Begin by using the finest grain clay you have. While porcelain is best, I used fine-grain white stoneware with good results. Shape the exterior of the mold by rolling or tapping on a cloth surface. To make it easier to hold on to, make the mold long or add a handle to the back. Flatten the front of it. If desired, add texture by pressing the mold on a textured cloth or other surface (figure 1).

Spray the object with a releasing agent such as cooking spray or WD-40 (figure 2). Center the object on the mold and press it onto the clay (figure 3). Carefully remove the object, and don't disturb the edges. Allow the mold to dry slowly then bisque fire (figure 4).

To apply, press a small ball of clay into the deep part of the mold (figure 5). Press extra clay on the rest of the mold (figure 6). Put a small amount of water, or slip, on the backside of sprig. With one hand, press the sprig on the pot from the outside. Apply pressure from both sides by using your other hand to press out toward the sprig from the inside (figure 7). If you put too much slop on the back of the sprig, it will ooze out and stick

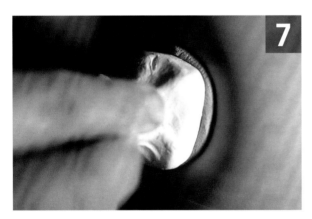

Detail shot of fired sprig decoration.

to the mold, which makes the mold stick to the pot. If this happens, just leave the mold in place for 5 minutes or so until it absorbs the moisture, then it will come right off. Molds can also stick when they become wet during use, in which case you'll need to stop and let the mold dry out before continuing.

Pressing the sprig deeply into the pot while the pot is still moist makes it less likely that it will come off in the dying process. This also gives the pot a look of spontaneity (figure 8).

Anne Fløche
Inspired by Terra Sigillata

by Lise Lotte Nielsen

"Arched Rectangular Plate," 21 inches in length, earthenware mixed with perlite, with terra sigillata.

Anne Fløche, a Danish ceramist, who for many years has worked as a studio potter, continues to go her own way. A minimalist, she hopes to bring out what is, in her opinion, the most important part of the clay medium: the texture. She refrains from using glazes. Instead, she works with intensely colored terra sigillata fired at a low temperature. The color of the clay itself also can be seen.

Fløche's works are often square forms made of slabs. There are plates, bottles, tiles, flat or curved tables, pots, and bowls which seem to be made of wood or cardboard due to their raw, dry, baked surfaces.

As a whole, her work seems strongly related to archaic Egyptian art, but there are no direct imitations. Fløche does not find it odious to seek inspiration from the history of civilization. According to her, this does not differ from the fact that we cook and eat food that we like from other cultures.

Fløche has acquired knowledge on her long journeys to Thailand, Korea, Japan and Mexico, as well as numerous trips to the museums of European cities. She is influenced by all mediums in their collections—painting, sculpture, textile, paper, glass, metal, wood, bone and composite materials.

Fløche is used to taking care of all the processes herself. She prepares the clay by mixing ball clay with local red clay and perlite. "It is an extremely slow process," says Fløche, "but it cannot be done differently, and it makes me happy when I open an exhibition and people say to me that looking at my ceramics makes them feel that they have plenty of time and gives them a sense of being at ease."

Translation by Pernille Holm Møller, MA, Århus, Denmark.

Square plate, 17 inches square, earthenware mixed with perlite, with terra sigillata.

Square box, 7 inches in height, earthenware mixed with perlite, with terra sigillata.

Square plate, 17 inches square, earthenware mixed with perlite, with terra sigillata.

Terra Sigillata Technique

by Anne Fløche

Terra sigillata is a very old and very simple material used by the Greeks and Romans. They used it to create burnished red-and-black wares fired at low temperatures—1650°–1830°F.

I fire higher, to 2010°F, because I find that my works are too fragile otherwise. There is a balance to maintain, however, because many colors become dull and dense if the firing temperature is too high. I apply the terra sigillata to bone-dry clay with a brush—broad brushes are particularly useful.

Fløche Terra Sigillata

Ball Clay	19.0%
China Clay.	77.0
Bentonite	3.5
Deflocculant	0.5
	100.0%

To this basic recipe, I add coloring oxides or stains, as one would with an ordinary slip.

I realize that I construct my slips in so many ways (even adding sand sometimes) that some might say that it is not really terra sigillata anymore. I suppose this might be true, but it is a very simple way of working, and I have not had many technical problems. I also do not leave my clay to settle, as is typical with terra sigillata, to obtain the finest grains. Many of the materials I use are so fine that this is not necessary. Only when I use a raw, local clay or a stoneware clay with grog do I leave it to settle and separate into layers. Fundamentally, the china clay can be replaced by any other clay: local clays, stoneware clays, etc. Each clay has its own nuances.

Some clays I use on their own, rather than using them in the recipe; however, nonplastic clays may peel. If this happens, I add more ball clay. Peeling may also occur if the terra sigillata is applied too thick.

My clay body is very coarse, so the terra sigillata sticks well to the surface. A very fine clay might pose problems. If the clay body is too fine, more grog can be added.

Small boxes, to 4 inches in height, earthenware mixed with perlite, with terra sigillata, by Anne Fløche.

Scratching the Surface
A Guide to Sgraffito

by Wayne Bates

The word sgraffito is derived from the Italian word graffito, a drawing or inscription made on a wall or other surface (graffito also gave us the word graffiti). Graffito is past participal of sgraffire, which means "to scratch." So the word sgraffito basically means to scratch and create a graphic or an image. In ceramics, sgraffito is a technique of ornamentation in which a surface layer is incised to reveal a ground of contrasting color.

I use sgraffito to get a clean line without masking or rulers, and I do more cutting than scraping. I use a handmade tool that is thin and cuts smoothly. I cut when the piece is stiff leather hard, which makes straight lines possible. If the piece is bone dry, the cut will be jagged and brittle. If the piece is too soft, the tool raises the edge of the cut and makes a higher ragged edge.

If your clay has grog in it, or anything coarser than fine sand, you won't get a smooth cut. I use a rubber-tipped air tool and a soft cosmetic brush to blow or brush off the cuttings. The cut pieces are still moist enough to stick if you touch them to the surface, so they should be removed frequently. You can use a thin coat of wax resist to protect light-colored areas from dark cuttings. The wax resist will burn off in the bisque.

Ball clays are used for engobes because they are the most plastic clays and shrink the most allowing more room in the recipe for non-plastic color, frit, modifiers and fillers. Frit is used to bind the coating to the surface and to increase the interface with the pot and the glaze.

Plates, 10 inches square, sgraffito decoration with clear glaze fired to cone 5.

 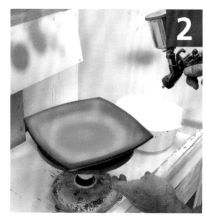 

I use an automotive-detail-type spray gun to apply engobes and glazes. It has a smaller fan size than the full-size gun, has good volume and is much faster than an airbrush. It's a high volume/low pressure (HVLP) gun and it produces less overspray. I use a large HLVP spray gun for the cover glazes because of its high volume.

CAUTION

Overspray is hazardous. The engobe spray contains silica, which can be harmful if inhaled. Wear a mask, and make sure your booth has an exhaust system.

Wollastonite is used to add calcium so the chrome-tin colors will work, and flint is used as a filler and stabilizer for colors that flux the mix. I mix the engobes thoroughly and screen them through an 80-mesh sieve. Most of my colors come from commercial glaze stains although not all commercial stains will work, but if you think of engobes as being closer to glazes than slips, additives can help produce the right colors. Changes in the frit affects how fluid an engobe is and how it works with the glaze. It can also produce a vitreous, glazelike surface. Changes in the amount of ball clay will make the engobe more or less plastic and change whether it goes on very wet pieces or bone-dry pieces.

I use a matt and a shiny glaze to cover the engobes on the face of the pieces and these two glazes are what I call "color friendly." To get as many colors as possible, they have to work with the chrome-tin colors, i.e., the reds, pinks and purples. The molecular recipe has to have three times more calcium than boron for these to work. They have that ratio and will produce the right color with all my engobes. I do use barium for what it does for the colors and for the matt. The potential problem with it has to do with the heavy metals and the possibility of leaching. From what I can find out, if a glaze has less than 15% barium in the percentage composition, it will not promote leaching. From the tests I have done, the glazes that I now use do not promote leaching when used over the engobes. I do use a liner glaze for liquid containers and I don't use the solid color glazes on eating surfaces.

I spray very wet, as if I'm pouring on a small stream of the glaze or engobe on the piece. The engobe sets quickly because the leather-hard piece can absorb some water, but too much engobe and the piece can collapse. If the engobe is too thick, it

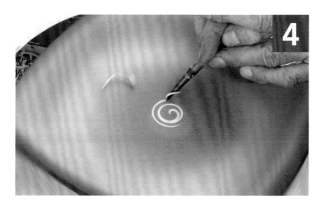

Place the platter on a foam rubber chuck on the wheel and create the center spiral as the wheel turns.

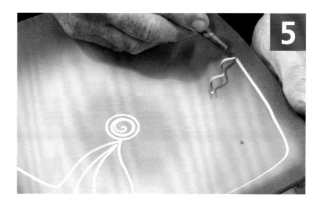

Move the platter to a banding wheel and work freehand.

Scrape off large areas last using the flat side of a rib.

Cross-hatching is done with a serrated tool.

makes the color and the glaze crawl. Set the fan for a tall oval and overlap the spray by 50% with the piece on a banding wheel turning smoothly through the spray. Practice spraying with paper plates so you can cover the plate smoothly with no bare spots or dusty areas.

The four colors of this color set are Black, French Green, Chartreuse and Crimson and are applied from dark to light (figures 1–2). The spray adds water to the piece and it must dry to the leather hard state before it can be carved. When dry enough, store the pieces on cloth on top of plastic,

and and place cloth over them to prevent condensation from the plastic marring the color (figure 3).

First I create the center spiral and circle using a foam rubber chuck on the wheel (figure 4). All the other lines are done freehand on a banding wheel (figure 5).

The scraping of the larger white spaces is done last, when the piece is even harder. I try to take off only the layer of color (figure 6). I use the the tool tip to make a sort of ditch that you can scrape to or from to make the larger white areas. I use the flat side of a rib to make the larger cuts.

There will be some edges that can be felt, and glazes will break away from these edges, but the glaze will fill in to make it smoother than when cut. Small nicks and cuts can be patched, but the spray overlaps are very hard to color match, so it is best to avoid mistakes! When almost bone dry, use 0000-grade steel wool to lightly smooth some of the cuts and to remove small bits of color.

Cross-hatching is another way of exposing the white of the porcelain and is done with a serrated-edge tool (figure 7). I add black dots of engobe using a squeeze bottle. When all the carving is done, the piece is air-dried then bisque fired, then a clear satin matt or a shiny glaze is sprayed on the front and solid color glazes on the back.

Tools

My sgraffito tool tips are made from the main spring of a pocket watch. The spring metal is thin and strong, doesn't have to be sharpened and keeps the same feel as it wears away. To make the tip, cut a piece of spring, heat it with a small torch and bend it to the shape you want. A small rounded point is used for the line cutting tips, and a broader rounder tip for large cuts. Glue the tip with Elmers glue into the brass ferrel of the trimming tool and allow it to harden. Lightly heating the ferrel softens the glue and the ferrel can be removed and another tip glued into the tool. For ribs, cut them with tin snips from sheets of metal and flatten the edges, making two square edges for scraping (do not sharpen the edges). You can also cut serrated-edge ribs with the snips.

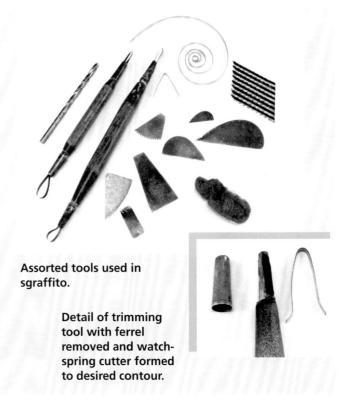

Assorted tools used in sgraffito.

Detail of trimming tool with ferrel removed and watch-spring cutter formed to desired contour.

Recipes

Sgraffito techniques can be a lot of fun, especially with a large color palette of engobes. Most of my colors come from commercial glaze stains. Frits, fillers and retardants are added, depending on the colorant used. The following engobes are mixed with Mason stains.

Engobes

UBL-45 Black
C&C Clay*	50 %
Ferro Frit 3195	20
Black #6600	30
	100 %

UR-31 Crimson
C&C Clay	50 %
Ferro Frit 3134	20
Wollastonite	10
Crimson #6006	20
	100 %

UG-35 French Green
C&C Clay	50 %
Ferro Frit 3134	15
Wollastonite	10
French Green #621	25
	100 %

UG-41 Chartreuse
C&C Clay	50 %
Ferro Frit 3134	20
Chartreuse #6236	30
	100 %

UBL-41 Light Blue Black
C&C Clay*	60 %
Nepheline Syenite	10
Wollastonite	10
Flint	10
Black #6616	10
	100 %

UG -69 Turquoise Green
C&C Clay	50 %
Wollastonite	10
Ferro Frit 3134	20
Turquoise #6393	20
	100 %

UBR-17 Seal Brown
C&C Clay	40 %
Nepheline Syenite	20
Wollastonite	10
Seal Brown #6153	30
	100 %

UB-18 Teal Blue
C&C Clay	60 %
Ferro Frit 3134	30
Teal #6305	10
	100 %

UR-28 Dot Red
C&C Clay	50 %
Wollastonite	20
Ferro Frit 3134	10
Crimson #6006	20
	100 %

UBL-46 Blue Black
C&C Clay	50 %
Nepheline Syenite	10
Silica	10
Black #6616	30
	100 %

UB 22-Turquoise Blue
C&C Clay	50 %
Ferro Frit 3134	10
Wollastonite	10
Zircopax	10
Turquoise #6390	20
	100 %

UP-49 Hot Pink
C&C Clay	40 %
Ferro Frit 3134	40
Pink #6020	20
	100 %

UP-34 Coral
C&C Clay	50 %
Ferro Frit 3134	10
Wollastonite	10
Coral #6090	30
	100 %

UGR-10 Silver Gray
C&C Clay	60 %
Ferro Frit 3134	10
Silica	10
Silver #6530	20
	100 %

UPR-32 Deep Orchid
C&C Clay	50 %
Nepheline Syenite	10
Deep Orchid #6303	30
Wollastonite	10
	100 %

UY-38 Hot Yellow
C&C Clay	50 %
Nepheline Syenite	10
Ferro Frit 3134	10
Wollastonite	10
Yellow #6481	20
	100 %

UW-1 White
C&C Clay	30 %
Nepheline Syenite	20
Ferro Frit 3134	10
Wollastonite	10
White #6700	30
	100 %

UB-7 Peacock Blue
C&C Clay	40 %
Nepheline Syenite	10
Peacock Blue #6396	40
Wollastonite	10
	100 %

UPR-31 Pansy Purple
C&C Clay	50 %
Nepheline Syenite	10
Wollastonite	13
Pansy Purple #6385	27
	100 %

*C&C clay is a ball clay. If not available, another ball clay may be used, but the results may vary. Although formulated for cone 6, many of these will work at higher and lower temperatures.

Recipes

Glazes

The following glaze recipes can be used over the engobes, but they can also be tinted with stains.

R-1030 Satin Matt*
Cone 5

Barium Carbonate	11 %
Wollastonite	15
Ferro Frit 3134	19
Nepheline Syenite	33
EPK Kaolin	16
Silica	6
	100 %

Similar to R-1015 but lower temperature. Will go shiny if fired higher. Top of my kiln.

R-1012 Satin Matt*
Cone 5

Barium Carbonate	11 %
Whiting	12
Ferro Frit 3134	17
Nepheline Syenite	44
EPK Kaolin	7
Silica	9
	100 %

Similar to R-1015 but lower temperature. Middle of my kiln.

R-1015 Satin Matt*
Cone 6

Barium Carbonate	16 %
Wollastonite	15
Ferro Frit 3134	13
Nepheline Syenite	33
EPK Kaolin	14
Silica	9
	100 %

G-19 Shiny Clear
Cone 6

Wollastonite	30 %
Ferro Frit 3195	30
EPK Kaolin	20
Silica	20
	100 %

Color friendly base, will produce shiny versions of most of the Mason stain colors. Can be used as a liner glaze, unlikely to produce leaching.

Frosty Matt
Cone 6

Barium Carbonate	22%
Lithium Carbonate	5
Nepheline Syenite	60
EPK Kaolin	8
Silica	5
	100 %

High alkaline, distinct color characteristics, crystalline sugar like surface, turns copper turquoise, brightens most colors.

*Contains barium. Can produce leaching when used with heavy metals. No claims made for success or safety.

Surface Etching
Wax and Water

by Ryan McKerley

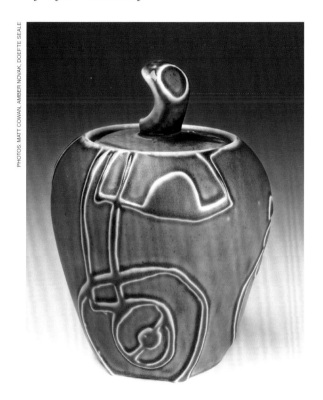

PHOTOS: MATT COWAN, AMBER NOVAK, DOEFTE SEALE

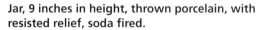

Jar, 9 inches in height, thrown porcelain, with resisted relief, soda fired.

Jar, 12 inches in height, thrown and altered porcelain, soda fired.

These pots are not carved in the traditional sense. The patterns are created by painting melted Gulf Wax (parafin) onto the surface of a bone dry vessel. I then scrub the unwaxed areas with a very wet sponge. The exposed clay erodes away as it is scrubbed, leaving a smooth depression. As I am scrubbing, I use a caliper to periodically check to make sure the wall isn't getting too thin. This body of work is thrown with Coleman porcelain. This clay body doesn't mind big differences in wall thickness.

I add a small amount of motor oil to the wax to help it flow off the brush. Too much oil will make the wax soft causing it to wash away with the clay. If the wax goes somewhere I don't want it to, I carve it away with a metal trimming tool.

Soda firing highlights the edges of the patterns and alters the glazes from side to side. The recessed areas of the surface receive less soda glaze, which creates further contrast. Copper glazes surprise me every firing, adding a little chance to this tedious process.

Recipes

Green to Black
Cone 10

Bone Ash.	5.5%
Dolomite	17.3
Whiting	7.0
Custer Feldspar	35.1
EPK Kaolin.	35.1
	100.0%
Add: Copper Carbonate.	9.4%
Tin Oxide.	3.4%

This glaze will be matt black when applied thick and soda fired in oxidation or reduction. A thin application combined with light soda glaze coverage can produce pumpkin oranges next to olive greens.

Val's Blue Black
Cone 8–10

Whiting	34 %
Custer Feldspar	31
EPK Kaolin.	25
Silica	10
	100%
Add: Copper Carbonate.	4%
Tin Oxide.	4%

This glaze has never been blue in my soda kiln. A thin coating almost always turns jade green. I prefer a thick coating of this glaze with lots of soda. The side of the pot facing away from the soda spray can be matt pink or green with black on the edges. The other side can go light green or black or both.

Vase, 9 inches in height, thrown and altered porcelain, soda fired.

Surface Etching
Resist and Mist

by Roger Graham

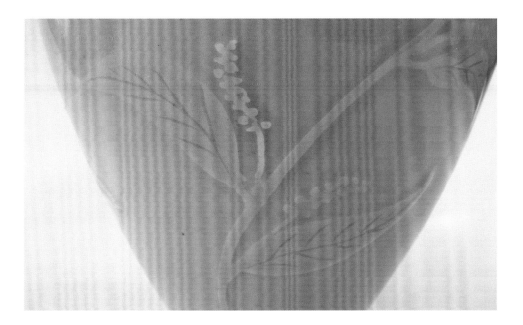

Last year while traveling, I bought a delightful porcelain pot with a delicate raised pattern on the outside, carved with infinite patience, or so I thought. "Not at all," the potter informed me, "It's water etching." Then he gave me a brief outline of how it's done.

Back home in the studio, I followed up on his technique. It opened up a whole new realm of possibilities. and some pleasant surprises. The process is so quick and the unprotected clay washes away so fast, that it's possible to etch to a depth of a millimeter or more in less than a minute and follow a wax outline precisely.

What kind of water spray you may ask? I use the ordinary gravity-feed spray gun used for applying glazes, but wound up the air pressure to about 100 psi instead of the usual 40. It was adjusted for a fine widespread spray and held about 2 inches from the pot. All of this was done on a banding wheel in a spray booth, but you could go outside and use a garden hose adjusted to a fine mist. Truly, it's as easy as that.

While you may expect the water spray to undercut the wax— just as sandblasting undercuts a stencil—the pattern remains crisply defined; even thin, fine lines survive undamaged. You might also expect the constant water spray to reduce the unfired clay to a soggy mess, but this hasn't been a problem, even with thinly thrown delicate pots. If you work swiftly, the whole procedure takes only a minute or two and the lower edge of the inverted pot, which would soften first, needs only a gentle blotting with a soft sponge.

Process

Produce work for this process using smooth, fine-grained clay. Allow it to dry to the bone-dry stage. Paint a design on the pot using wax resist and a fine brush. Adding food dye to the wax makes it easier to see where you've been (figure 1).

Invert the pot and suspend it on a pedestal or chuck. The rim of the pot needs to overhang the pedestal so water can drip into a catch basin (figure 2).

This pot was given a smooth, even coat of blue slip (1.5% cobalt oxide), just enough to cover the area where the design will go. The simple plant motif was painted on, using wax emulsion heavily loaded with dye so the narrow brushstrokes were easy to see.

Apply a fine spray of water. The water will wash away clay that is not protected by the wax. Gently blot away water droplets from the rim with a soft sponge (figure 3) to prevent the rim from disintegrating. Warm air from a hair dryer speeds up the return to crisp dryness.

Note: When using colored slips, don't forget that the rinse water is now contaminated with the slip's colorants, so dispose of it accordingly.

When the pot is dry again, or nearly dry, you can pick it up and refine the details if necessary. These details are easily added by hand with a pointed tool after the water-etched pattern has dried. If you're not satisfied with an outline of part of your design, just scrape it away. It's easy to make minor repairs, just don't get carried away (figure 4).

The edges of the pattern remain sharp and jagged lines can be touched up with a pointed tool if deemed necessary. Extra details like leaf veins can be drawn now, while the pot is still a bit damp, so the scriber makes a smooth clean line without breaking out little chips and crumbs.

Figure 5 shows what to expect with bits of grog or grit in the clay. To avoid an uneven surface, use porcelain or a very smooth, clean stoneware.

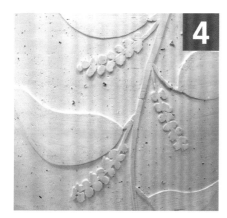

Spray a thin coat of dark slip (10% red iron oxide) and allow to dry. Then, as in the original process, paint on a design using wax resist, then you will want to suspend the pot upside down on a pedestal. Use the water spray to wash away the brown slip exposing the white clay.

There will be times when you want a basket-weave effect, where one strand of the pattern has to pass behind or in front of another. In this example, the fish's tail is behind one strand of weed, but the head is in front of another. This technique was done using a pointed knife to scrape away a little clay where it matters.

A finished pot with a cobalt blue eucalyptus motif and clear overglaze fired to cone 10.

Pièce de Résistance

by Russel Fouts

**"There It Begins,"
19 in. in diameter,
handbuilt earthen-
ware decorated with
tape and paper resist,
and terra sigillata,
smoke-fired in an
electric kiln.**

I smoke fire in an electric kiln using newspaper in aluminum foil
saggars. Since the combustible
material is trapped inside the foil,
there is almost no movement of the
smoke so it is prevented from making patterns on the pots. To com-
pensate for this, I rely on resists to
create interesting surfaces. But the
problem is that traditional resists—
like wax or latex—prove unsatis-
factory because they resist too well
and don't allow for "accidents" to
happen. Traditional resists work by
creating barriers that repel liquids
like slips, glazes, washes and over/

underglazes, but I'm also interested
in controlling how much and where
my work absorbs smoke.

Rethinking the concept of a resist and what makes it work, or not
work, opens up a whole new world of
possibilities for resist decoration. My
efforts are now entirely directed toward the use of "permeable" resists.
Resists that sort of resist and sort of
don't; that block while still allowing
some interaction with the surface
underneath. Once you understand
how resists create barriers, you can
broaden your resist decorating "palette" and use their special characteristics in your work.

Non-traditional Water Resists

What materials repel water? Think
about all the different materials
that contain waxes, oils or greases,
including the oil from your skin.
Soften any of these resists by warm-
ing them a little and the quality of
the line changes. Here are some
hard and soft resist materials you
can try.

"Beaten Bowl," 19 in. in diameter, handbuilt earthenware with wax and soda resist, and terra sigillata, smoke fired in an electric kiln.

Hard Resists

- Lipstick—a nice greasy line
- Eyebrow pencil
- Wax crayon—scratchy line
- Grease pencil or china marker
- Chunk of wax or a candle—produces a very similar line to the china marker, and you can adjust the width of the line by choosing bigger or smaller pieces
- Oil pastels—similar line to wax but fatter, and you can use it sideways.
- Bar of soap
- Leftover chocolate—(As a Belgian, this is a real sacrifice for me.) different kinds of chocolate make different kinds of lines; the harder, the more scratchy, the softer, the fatter the line.

Soft Resists

- Full strength white glue, wood glue or any acrylic glue—trail like slip or dilute for brushing
- Acrylic floor polish—as the ads state "waterproofs and resists black heel marks"
- Acrylic artist's medium
- Liquid beeswax—nice to decorate with and works in a pinch for waxing bottoms or feet
- Paste wax or Vaseline—good

for smudgy marks when applied with a cloth or fingers

■ Left over oil-based creams on your dresser

■ Any oils—they can be brushed, smudged or spattered

Paper Resists

While paper resists won't work on bisque where I do most of my decoration, tape does and comes in many different forms and widths. Drafting and pin striping tapes come in extremely fine widths and are very flexible. Stickers are also an option. If you want a shape or thickness in a tape or sticker that isn't available, cut the exact shape you want out of paper, glue it to the pot with diluted white glue and smooth it down with a rubber or foam roller. Or stick the edges of your paper cutout down with a border of tape. You could also cut your design out of self adhesive shelf paper or even masking tape.

Colored Resists

The cuerda seca technique, which originated in Persia and eventually moved to Spain, is the technique of creating an open design using wax, oil or grease containing manganese or iron. The defined areas are then filled with fluid, i.e., colored glazes. When the work is fired, the resist keeps the colors separated and leaves a black or brown line between them.

■ Expand on this technique by adding any under- or overglaze colorant to any of the liquid resists mentioned above.

■ Many of the hard resists such as crayons, pastels and lipsticks are colored with the same oxides used in ceramics, and often leave a colored trace when they melt.

Hard Resists. Chocolate, crayons, oil pastels, bar paraffin, candles, china marker, stick paraffin, soap bar and lipstick. Note: "Hard" resists work well on soft, raw glaze or slip, sprayed or brushed with a solution of CMC gum or gelatin to harden the surface. I use a solution of VeeGum C diluted with water until it can be easily sprayed.

Masking Materials. Newspaper, various masking tapes, sisal (fuzzy string), stickers, plastic wrap, various cotton strings and "lining" tape.

Liquid Resists. Latex, liquid beeswax, white glue, white glue diluted with water, salad oil, hot wax, cream shoe polish, acrylic medium and paste beeswax.

- Paper cutouts or torn strips soaked in a solution of diluted white glue and a colorant also leave behind a trace of the colorant contained in the glue.

Pressure Resists

Think of tie dying. Wrapping different materials around your piece can provide different effects.

- Tightly wrapped string, rubber bands, or even plastic wrap (rolled into a "string" or left flat) resist water to a differing extent.

- "Fuzzy" strings (e.g., sisal) can leave a distinctive mark. If the string is absorbent, try soaking it in terra sigillata, a colorant or even a liquid resist, squeezing it out a bit to avoid drips. Carefully wrap the pot with it and then apply further decoration, slip, glaze or terra sigillata.

- Use strings made of natural materials that can either be removed before firing or left to burn out in the kiln.

- Experiment with absorbent and nonabsorbent materials. Try using string or rubber bands to hold open-weave cloth against the pot.

- Think of those lovely finger marks left behind by the potter in the glaze around the foot of a dipped bowl. Make different kinds of marks with your fingers or hands to block the application of dipped, sprayed or spattered materials.

Smoke Resists

Clays and glazes can resist smoke. For smoke resist to work, fire the work first to at least the point of sintering to seal them, usually a bisque temperature. Once sealed, any of the following will resist against further applications of colorants, terra sigillatas or glazes.

- Terra sigillata is not just about shine. Since most terra sigillatas are made with low firing clays, they keep the underlying body from absorbing the smoke. They take on some smoke themselves but they'll absorb less than the body underneath.

- Glazes form a barrier to smoke and can also be used to add color. An example of this is a white crackle raku glaze.

- A saturated solution of sodium carbonate (washing soda) and water, diluted sodium silicate, or any salt solution form a primitive glaze, sealing the surface of the pot against the effects of smoking.

- Metal foils, like aluminum, can be another interesting resist against smoke. Try covering the whole or part of the pot and cutting holes in the foil to let smoke in where you want. They can also be used as pressure resists or as nonpermeable paper resists when stuck down with tape or removable glue.

- A simple, thin slab of moist clay applied to the side of a pot also works as a resist against smoke.

Testing Alternative Resists

The items tested are listed at the end of each row. The first column shows the resist applied to a bisque surface. In the middle column, the tiles have been dipped in a soda solution on the left side and dipped in a $1/10$ terra sigillata and soda solution on the right side, leaving the center portion untreated. In the third column, the tiles have been fired to 900°C with newspapers and wrapped in heavy-duty aluminium foil saggars, in a well-ventilated electric kiln. After firing, a stripe of acrylic floor finish was applied to show how color and contrast can be enhanced.

Smoke Resists
- Brushed soda ash solution
- Cut make-up pads dipped in soda solution
- Paper dipped in soda solution
- Sponged soda solution
- Spattered soda solution using a masque
- Brushed terra-sigillata and soda solution
- Brushed straight terra sigillata

Waxy Resists
- Lipstick
- Oil pastel
- Oil pastel sideways
- Crayon
- Crayon sideways
- China marker
- Sacrificed chocolate
- Bar soap

  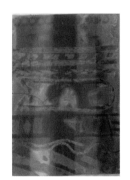

Masking Materials
- Hole reinforcements
- Mask cut from postal sticker
- Thin masking tape
- Thin masking tape torn
- Zigzag of tape
- Paper masque stuck down with tape
- Masking tape cut as a stencil
- Flexible "lining" tape
- Torn strips of newspaper dipped in glue and terra sigillata and stuck down

Liquid Resist
- Brushed beeswax
- Brushed salad oil
- Brushed diluted white glue
- Trailed and feathered white glue
- Latex with a cutout
- Smudged hand cream
- Brushed cream shoe polish

Application

Treat liquid or soft resist materials like any other decorating material. They are the same as oxides, colorants, terra sigillatas, slips or glazes, and you can use any means you think of to apply them to a surface. Feel free to dip, pour, spatter (one of my favorites), spray, splash, squirt or brush as inspiration directs you. Also, consider that "bad" tools can often leave the most interesting marks. Look for orphaned tools; balding brushes, spitting sprayers, decrepit sponges, ragged bits of cloth or loose bits of string. How about a mop? Not a mop brush but the hoary, old, string mop standing in the corner.

Safety

Most of the materials discussed are safe to use. All natural materials should burn out safely in your kiln although you need a good venting system if you're firing indoors. Paper, tape and natural strings can either be left in place or removed as you wish. Left on, the ash residue can leave interesting traces. Plastics like acrylics and floor finishes require adequate ventilation. Trailed white glue and pin striping tape should be removed before firing. The soda solution, applied directly to the surface of the work, causes only a very localized effect and is safe to use in any kiln.

WARNING: Manganese fumes from kilns have been linked to certain neurological disorders.

Smoke resists. (Left to right) Diluted terra sigillata with soda solution, straight terra sigillata, diluted terra sigillata and soda solution.

Applicators. Assorted "bad" brushes, sponge brush, toothbrush, assorted textured sponges and make-up pads.

Conclusion

I hope you're getting the idea. The list can go on and on. Basically ANYTHING that makes a barrier against water or smoke works in some way and each one has its own special character. Think about trying these techniques at different stages of the pot's or the decoration's development. There are a lot of ideas here but I seriously doubt that I've exhausted all the possibilities.

The chart on the following page reveals the effects different resists have on a clay surface that has been smoke fired in a saggar.

Creating a
Weathered Patina

by Dennis Maust

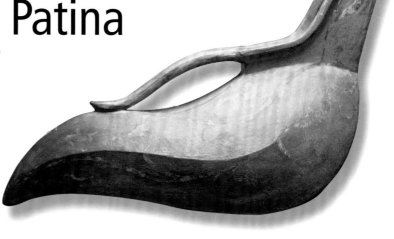

In my studio I've employed several techniques for antiquing or creating the appearance an aged surface. I have always been drawn to surfaces that show their weathered history and am intrigued by images that suggest rather than spoon feed a message. I discover new possibilities each time I try this technique and maybe that's what has kept me using these methods year after year.

Newspaper and Slip Technique

This technique involves the repeated application of different colored slips using newspaper as an application tool. Brush colored slip on newspaper to place on a leather-hard piece (figure 1). Smooth the slipped newspaper out somewhat. Leaving some wrinkles adds to the texture (figure 2). When the paper has been smoothed to your satisfaction, peel it back off (figure 3). Immediately paint a different-colored slip on the same piece of newspaper, and apply it to the piece in the same or different location (figure 4). Repeating these steps using slightly different colors of slip builds up complex, random surface design.

Lay the newspaper on the patterned mold.

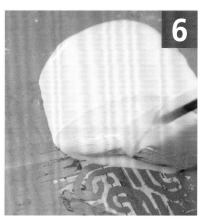

Paint another layer of a different
slip on the newspaper.

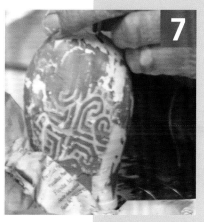

Apply to the pot, smooth out and
peel away to reveal the pattern.

Press Mold and Slip Technique

I sometimes use patterned plaster press molds to vary the surface, making it more interesting (figures 5-7). Before laying the slipped newspaper on my pot, I lay it on the plaster mold and peel it off. I then paint another layer of slip over the slipped newspaper and apply it to the pot. Peeling this off again leaves an imperfect image of the pattern but leaves the impression parts were worn off over time.

Other Techniques

On some pieces, I build up many layers of this random slip decoration. Then, on the areas I find most appealing, I wax resist and spray areas of solid color slip or oxide wash to create a sense of shards having been put back together (the plain color being the part fabricated to support the "found shards"). A variation on this has been to draw a more intentional design with wax resist over an area of layered slip (after the piece has been bisqued) and then spraying a glaze or terra sigillata over it.

I have varied the thickness of the slip and at times dried the slip-covered newspaper, crumpling it before painting the subsequent layer of slip. Each variation gives a different effect, sometimes a marbleized appearance or that of peeling paint.

Slip trailing on newspaper, then painting another layer of slip over it before applying to the pot, also enables one to work on a flat horizontal surface for gestural work that may be difficult on upright curved surfaces.

After bisque firing I often brush oxide washes over the surface and then sponge off. The edges of the various layers of slip show up more giving the surface more depth under a glaze.

I have also used this technique with terra sigillata on bone dry burnished ware. The resulting work tends to be smoother and more convincing as something ancient.

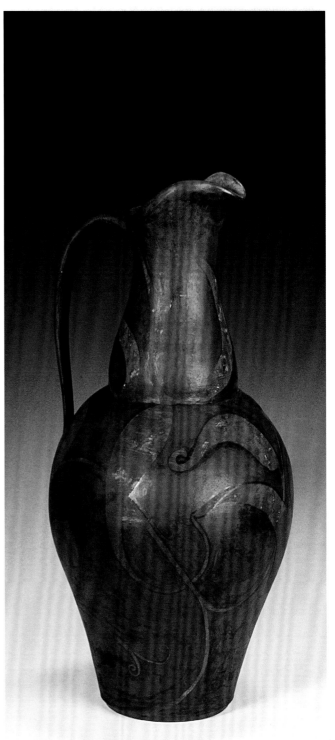

Top left: Applying an oxide wash to a piece that had been painted with a wax-resist pattern. Bottom right: Wiping off the oxide. Right: Finished work created using that technique.

Chris Gryder
Surfaces from Silt

by Dori DeCamillis

A lot of Gryder's work is comprised of special commissions like the one for the Meacham residence in Malvern, Pennsylvania. "This allows for greater freedom in developing large compositional themes," Gryder says. 7½ feet in width, silt-cast stoneware with colored terra sigillatas and dark clay wash, fired to cone 3.

Chris Gryder began his exploration of art by studying architecture. A sincere and dedicated commitment to the subject led to his acquaintance with artists, methods and concepts that later became the inspiration for his work in sculpture and clay. From the visionary designs of Antonio Gaudi and the philosophy of Louis Sullivan, to experimental work in mold making for architectural pieces, Gryder

pieced together a singular aesthetic and an uncommon process of sculpture making.

During his undergraduate work he discovered the work of Gaudi. His eyes were opened to a new world of architectural form. Gaudi incorporated ceramics in his architectural surfaces. Ornament was not only used, it encompassed entire buildings. It *was* the building. While Gaudi's work gets categorized as

Art Nouveau, it fully transcended the movement by taking the typical flowing, plantlike forms so popular at the time and using them not only as motif but as architectural framework. He was a sculptor on a very grand scale. Gryder responded to everything about the work: the diversity of form, the hands-on quality of execution, the acceptance of ornament, the abundance of references to the natural world.

For three years, Gryder worked in the field of architecture until a five-year stint in the desert of Arizona turned his head to the world of sculpture. He lived and worked on Paolo Soleri's project "Arcosanti," which had been developing prototypes for urban ideas since the 1970s in a clay studio and bronze foundry 65 miles north of Phoenix. While Gryder worked there building architectural pieces, he overwhelmingly responded to building with his hands. Working in the ceramic studio he gained rudimentary technical knowledge and started playing with the idea of making molds in the negative. With memories of Gaudi emerging, he began an interest in making organic sculptural forms.

Gryder began graduate work at Rhode Island School of Design with ideas and inspiration fueled by his recent explorations at Arcosanti. The most striking aspect of his art making during his graduate years was the atypical process he used to create vessels. All pieces are fashioned in the negative. Explained in basic terms, he first builds a box

and fills it with packed silt. With his hands and simple tools, he carves a negative into the silt, which will become the exterior of the vessel. From there he pours commercial slip (with roughly the density of a thick milk shake) into the carved cavity. The slip dries slightly over several hours until Gryder scoops out all the slip that is still liquid. When the clay has dried completely he breaks the mold and has a completed greenware piece. The surface is then covered with neutral colors of terra sigillata.

The process is involved and time consuming, but appealing to Gryder. He explains that in a one-off single casting the artist doesn't have to concentrate time and energy on preparing the mold for repetitive use, a process of accommodation which often informs the piece visually. More freedom of design is allowed with a mold that dissolves after each piece. The procedure also offers the opportunity for more spontaneous and unexpected results.

Covering the outside of Gryder's vessels are odd protruding forms that travel in patterns. When aware of the artist's process, one can imagine the act of scooping that produces the curious structure and contour. Whether seeming to be strange botanical elements or grotesque geological formations, one is reminded somewhat of Gaudi. The surface is rough, like sand, with peculiar gatherings of hardened sediment tucked into the tight spaces between forms. Without knowing the process, a

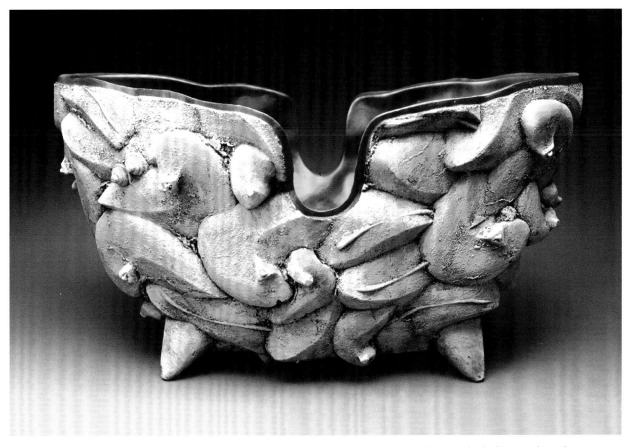

"Viscus Notch," 13 inches in height, silt-cast stoneware with colored terra sigillatas, dark clay wash and manganese glaze (interior), fired to cone 3. Gryder says his forming process is "akin to drawing in the dark."

seasoned clay enthusiast would be hard-pressed to understand how the extraordinary surface was achieved.

In contrast to the swelling forms, coarse texture and matt patina of the exterior, the inside finish is smooth and satiny, and a different color. The fervent dissimilarity of surface is entirely arresting, reminding one of a broken coconut or a sea creature with an open shell. Historically vessels have represented, among other things, the human soul. Gryder's pieces allude to this symbolism with their harsh, seemingly protective

outer layer which opens to reveal a velvety interior.

Vessels were Gryder's primary focus in grad school, but he also dabbled in tiles using the same process. After graduating and finding a following for his work, tiles became more of a focus, and eventually their popularity and his interest in them pushed them into the forefront of his production.

Like the exterior of the vessels, Gryder's tile surfaces have a sandstone-like quality. The aesthetic of Gryder's tiles unite his former train-

Beauty from Silt

by Chris Gryder

The natural world is often the source for my work, but the inspiration goes beyond simply translating this visual world. My technique is inspired by and akin to an actual physical process within the natural world which leads to fossils. The latin "fossus" translates "having been dug up," and I similarly excavate my clay works from sediment. A fossil is the trace of the remains of some organic body, creature or plant, within sediment. I likewise create trace carvings in the sediment or silt. I build form via the aegis of negative space. A reductive approach, an intricate cavity is dug in the silt which ultimately acts as a dissolvable one-off mold. The material I use to cast into is silt, a very fine sediment created as a result of alluvial action. It is basically comprised of about 70% fine sand and 30% clay. The sand can be thought of as very tiny building blocks and the clay in the mix acts as a mortar to bind the particles together when wet. The porosity of the silt mold allows the basic mechanics of slip casting to operate; the water in the liquid clay migrates into the mold leaving behind slightly more solidified layer of clay at the surface.

This layer becomes thicker as the mold remains filled. Once the desired thickness is achieved, the remaining slip is removed leaving behind a clay shell. As the clay dries and reaches a leather hard state, it can be excavated from the crumbling and dissolving silt mold. This casting technique sacrifices the advantages of multiple castings in favor of rich encrusted and serendipitous surfaces that can be carved directly without concern for undercuts and seams. This is a studio mold and casting technique that approaches the immediacy of drawing rather than the precise methodical planning often associated with mold making.

"Swirl Relief," 9 inches in height, silt-cast stoneware with colored terra sigillatas, dark clay wash and manganese glaze (interior), fired to cone 3, by Chris Gryder.

ing and influences in modern design with his passion for the sensual and primordial. Furthermore, the two-dimensional aspect of tiles leaves room for more pictorial and narrative exploration. The tiles as a group manifest themselves in large wall-relief constructions, often 8–10 feet in length. Gryder starts by developing the piece linearly, focusing on overall form. The divisions of space could represent primitive ceremonial diagrams, molecular models, or planetary trajectories, conjuring associations with the metaphysical and the scientific. Possible horizons divide night and day, sea and land, earth and sky, above and underground. These divisions seem proportional and balanced enough to give the impression that the artist has used the Golden Mean for calculation. Indeed, a sense of the mathematical pervades the work, and is all the more emphasized by the grid formation of the tiles themselves. Like crop circles in a field of perfectly straight rows of corn, one wonders if an indecipherable map has been laid out, its function hidden behind its mysterious beauty.

Within the individual tiles are myriad abstract forms which reference, for the most part, the natural world. At first one is confident in deciphering leaf forms, but on closer examination leaves could be feathers, wings, or crystalline growth. A suggestion of insects, fruit, seeds and pods seems feasible. The eye can follow forms that insinuate ocean waves, branches on a tree, an-

"Pinwheel," 34 inches in width, silt-cast stoneware with colored terra sigillatas and dark clay wash, fired to cone 3. One of the challenges Gryder faces with his silt-casting technique is applying the colored washes and terra sigillata without marring the silt-textured surface.

imal trails, veins on a leaf, or water ripples. The rises in the relief hint at a possible model of a landscape. And while features of the natural world are hinted at, it wouldn't be far-fetched to see the spinning cogs and mechanisms of a moving contraption. The whole impression is one of liveliness and action.

Many of Gryder's influences reach far back into history, probably due to the proliferation of ornamental carved relief in primitive cultures. The artist's design arrangements and motifs recall Pre-Columbian architectural facades, especially Incan patterns and Mayan imagery. As in prehistoric cultures he frequently uses circular forms with layers radiating from a center like icons or mandalas. Added to these influences of design is the fact that the art of

early cultures now exhibits the damage of time. Gryder's technique lends a quality of aged or decayed stone, reminiscent of ancient ruins.

The success of Chris Gryder's work lies in his ability to combine and integrate so many opposing approaches to expression. With a seamless style he manages to mix the purity of modernism with a joyous celebration of profuse ornament, an ostensibly impossible task. His imagery invokes disparate ideas, from the analytical approach of science to the spiritual demonstrations of primitive culture. The work captures a feeling of the ancient and the new, the naïve and the sophisticated, spontaneity and order. Gryder's skill in encompassing and uniting divergent themes offers the viewer an exceptionally rich experience.

Marcy Neiditz
Transformation and Mutation

by Amy Norgaard

Marcy Neiditz imbues her ceramic sculpture and functional pottery with attributes that give them the sense of being alive. It is her love of organic form and textured surface that influences the art she creates.

Neiditz grew up in Cleveland and moved to Los Angeles. While there, she pursued a career in landscaping and horticulture, building on her interest in plants she developed from working for various landscape companies and plant nurseries. Eventually, she established her own interior landscape design business.

She's always finding new ways to challenge herself. Embracing her peculiar and unique technical and conceptual ideas, she pushes form and surface, merging the two as she builds in clay then glazes. She creates a union between organic forms and multifired surfaces that innately breathes life into her sculptures. In a balancing act of form and surface, she gives her work a quiet, yet rhythmic clarity.

Neiditz is interested in the transformation and mutation of plant life in her sculptures, which portray a disquieting uneasiness having plant, animal and/or human characteristics. Perhaps one sees branch, bone or flower forms in Neiditz's work, or perhaps one can stretch the imagination to see the microorganisms she is so interested in recreating. A multitude of references encourage contemplation. One of her impetuses is her fascination with polar opposites such as life and death, attraction and repulsion, growing and aging. She says, "These ingredients occupy my imagination and then become odd, quirky forms that suggest breathing, living organisms."

As she scrutinizes the conceptual

**"Life-Form Bacteria,"
20 inches in height,
handbuilt white
earthenware paper
clay, with glazes,
stains and oxides,
multifired to cone 04.**

content of her work, she becomes equally engaged in the physical process. It is her love of organic form that she focuses on when building petal by petal, leaf by leaf, almost molecule by molecule. Neiditz's process of building using a single clay "cell" that is repeated over and over develops a work that evolves naturally, and certainly references the growth of life.

Neiditz seeks a surface encrusted with texture so that it's no longer recognizable as a clay surface. The variations in her surface textures are both seductive and distressing. Layers of information create a history of process culminating in a representation of growing and aging, like tree rings or geological strata.

Teapot, 8 inches in height, handbuilt white earthenware paper clay, with glazes, stains and oxides, multifired to cone 04.

"Tea for Two," to 6 inches in height, wheel-thrown white earthenware and handbuilt white earthenware paper clay, with glazes, stains and oxides, multi-fired to cone 04.

She is inspired by the organic figurative works of fiber artist Magdalena Abakanowicz, the textured paintings of Anselm Kiefer and the simplistic forms of Martin Puryear's sculptures. Neiditz says, "tight, symmetrical, wheel-thrown vessels, like those tiny little weed pots made by Rose Cabot, are the origins of some of the forms I have developed." She looks at these tiny egg-like forms as the organisms that are multiplying in her sculptures. Her work shows the cyclical nature of her process, incorporating parts that use the cell-by-cell method, growing into or out of a well-proportioned volumetric form. They are smaller in scale than previous bodies of work, yet continue to demonstrate a love of ceramic glaze and glaze chemistry. Her work seldom leaves one wanting more surface exploration.

Neiditz's functional forms bring forth all that her sculptures contain and more, and her obsession with organic form is equally expressed. In her wonderful teapots, lidded jars and funky bottles, she never denies the sculptural elements. Fascinated with her encrusted glaze surface, she also incorporates two-dimensional patterns utilizing the ceramic surface as canvas.

Neiditz's sculptural and functional works synthesize a strange blending of the organic and extraterrestrial. Her exploration into the mysteries of the natural world is the beginning of the process. From there, she finds a platform to express her visual language and skill with clay.

"Bottle with Lid," 23 inches in height, handbuilt white earthenware paper clay, with glazes, stains and oxides, multifired to cone 04.

Her surfaces vary from wet to dry, giving the impression that the piece recently transformed into a living organism—one that has been buried or discovered underwater, then recently exposed to air, cleaned and invaded with fungus. Her interest and ideas about nature and plant life are transformed into cultivated artworks about life.

Surface variation begins with form

Marcy Neiditz's building techniques are hidden within her sculptures and usually lack typical process marks. She combines handbuilding techniques, such as pinching, coiling and slab building, with wheel throwing. For handbuilding, she mixes approximately 25% paper fibers into her white earthenware clay body and uses the same clay minus the paper fibers for wheel-thrown parts. Adding paper to the clay allows her to handbuild thin, yet sturdy, components.

Once the forms have been assembled and bisque fired, she focuses on creating a textured surface. She uses repeated firing of stains, glazes and oxides. Pulling a sculpture out of the kiln with one layer of glaze, Neiditz observes that there is more history to be revealed. She returns it to the glazing table, and then the kiln, again and again, until she is content. The key to her surfaces is nonuniformity in the wall thickness and glaze application. The water from the glaze absorbs rapidly into thicker areas of the sculpture, creating a thicker layer of glaze on the surface. In thinner areas, the glaze barely covers the surface. Other ceramists may find this problematic, but Neiditz has turned it into an advantage.

"Rusty Turquoise Life-Form," 15 inches in height, handbuilt white earthenware paper clay, with glazes, stains and oxides, multifired to cone 04, by Marcy Neiditz.

Creating Faux Surfaces

by Billie Mitchell

Baseballs and
football made from
two pinch pots and
paddled into shape.
The baseballs are
approximately
3 inches in diameter
and the football is
14 inches long.

A few years ago, many people thought my work was metal or leather because of the way the surface was treated. Their disbelief that my work was handbuilt from clay started my mind reeling with ideas. I began to pursue creating pieces that would capitalize on this accidentally stumbled-upon treatment. I am surrounded by inspiration and I now enjoy creating trompe l'oeil (literally: fool the eye) pieces on purpose. And they continue to fool people! Each new project begins with something that is familiar. I measure the original object and add 10% to the dimensions to allow for shrinkage. A couple of my favorite faux objects to make are baseballs and footballs. When creating base-balls, I choose to simulate the same dark leather I use on the footballs because the first baseballs were made of dark leather.

Process

For the baseballs and footballs, make pinch pots from very soft clay and put them together (figure 1). Paddle the form into a smooth ball or oval to get them to the approximate shape. Let them dry to a soft leather stage hard (figure 2).

Finish shaping and smoothing with a rubber rib and, if needed, roll the texture onto the surface with a "pony roller." For texture, I use crumpled up wax paper, a cut up old purse or faux leather from a fabric store. For a smooth leather look, I

Make two pinch pots 10% larger than the original object you are duplicating.

Assemble the two pinch pots and paddle the ball shape until round.

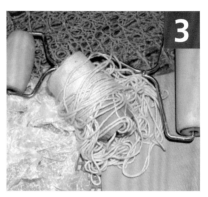

Pressing crumpled wax paper or rolling fake leather fabric or string into the surface are two ways to create a faux surface.

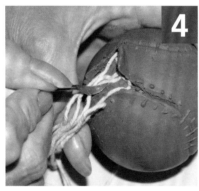

Put in seams and undercut exposed insides, then use string to make the inside texture of the baseball.

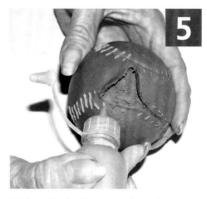

Make slip for laces and apply before leather hard.

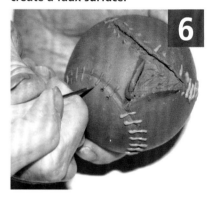

Put in holes for laces before they become leather hard.

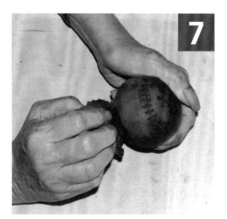

Apply stain to the entire surface. Make sure to get into all of the crevices for the right look.

rub the clay with my finger in a circular motion (figure 3). The cores of old baseballs were made of string or yarn, so I sometimes split them at the seams to give a more interesting effect and press string into the surface for texture (figure 4).

For baseballs, add laces using slip made from the same clay body (figure 5). Put the laces on before making the holes where the lace stitching would be (figure 6). Make some of the holes go all the way to the inside to keep the piece from blowing

The duffle bag with shoes shows the range of possibilities with this technique. Use colored clays arranged in patterns for duffle bags. It all depends on what you're making and the finished look you want. The duffle bag here measures 24 inches long by 20 inches in height and features faux clothes in contrasting clay. The shoes are a size 8.

up. For footballs, cut strips of clay from a thin slab made of contrasting clay.

After bisque firing, color the pieces with faux stain making sure to cover the entire surface. Wipe the piece off, leaving the stain in the crevices and folds (figure 7). This may take several attempts to get the desired effect. Sometimes I don't stir the stain since I want more of a wash; or I'll use the settled portion of the stain, as it's a lot stronger. I usually use a combination of the three effects on the same piece. Since pieces get darker the higher they are fired, the final firing temperature depends on how dark I want the final piece to be.

Photo credits: Bill Massey, Chris Bauman and Lou Hall.

Recipe

Mitchell's Faux Stain

Gerstley Borate	50%
Red Iron Oxide	50
	100%

Building Complex Surfaces with Multiple Firings

by Nicole Copel

Two teapots by Yoshiro Ikeda, showcasing his signature Crackle White glaze.

Yoshiro Ikeda has developed a process for making ceramic art that allows him to leave his work and respond to the unpredictable demands and responsibilities of a studio professor. His students can attest to the small space he occupies when working and the simplicity of his artistic tools. His workspace typically consists of a chair, a bag of clay, a handful of tools and a plastic bucket he uses as a work surface. In addition, he works in relatively short blocks of time.

He uses brushes to apply multiple layers of glazes, including his signature Crackle White glaze. This glaze has been formulated to separate into irregularly shaped beads, revealing the clay body below the glaze. The crackle glaze emphasizes textures and patterns unique to the surface treatment of his pieces.

Process

Yoshiro builds most of his sculptures and teapot using Soldate clay, which is bisque fired to cone 06. He then marks out compositional elements with a pencil (figure 1). After the surface design is drawn, he applies Crackle White Glaze to the sections where there are no markings using a hake brush (figure 2).

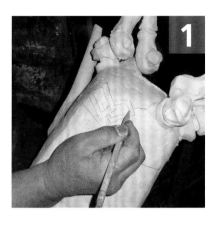
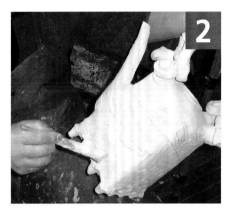

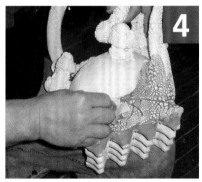

After the initial glaze application, Yoshiro draws a needle tool through the glaze to create expressive cut lines (figure 3). He then fires the piece to cone 02 in an electric kiln. After the first glaze firing, Yoshiro brushes his Black Glaze over the fired piece, filling deep crevices where the clay body is visible. After approximately twenty minutes, he wipes away the Black Glaze leaving it in the recessed areas (figure 4), then fires the piece to cone 03.

Because the high-fire clay is fired to a low temperature, it does not completely vitrify and is therefore able to absorb additional glaze.

Where the crackle glaze ends and the unglazed surfaces begin, Yoshiro applies a line of Matt Copper Blue Glaze with a brush (figure 5) and refires the piece to cone 03. Firing in between applications allows Yoshiro to see the results of the glazing before proceeding to the next glaze application and firing.

In this example, Yoshiro brushes Yellow Ochre and Iron Glaze onto the unglazed top of the piece and refires to cone 03 (figure 6). When he wants to achieve a more mottled effect, he uses a thick application of this glaze. Thinner applications result in a light brown shiny surface

Recipes

Crackle White Glaze
Cone 02

Magnesium Carbonate	33 %
Ferro Frit 3110.	67
	100 %
Add: Zircopax	11 %

Increasing the magnesium carbonate increases the dry crackle effect and fluxes (melts) the glaze.

Black Glaze
Cone 03

Nepheline Syenite	78 %
Ferro Frit 3110.	17
Ball Clay	5
	100 %
Add: Manganese Dioxide.	33 %
Bentonite	5 %

Caution: Manganese dioxide is toxic and is not suitable for food surfaces. Follow handling instructions from your supplier.

Matt Copper Blue Glaze
Cone 03

Whiting.	5 %
Lithium Carbonate.	22
Kaolin	15
Silica.	58
	100 %
Add: Copper Carbonate.	5 %
Bentonite	3 %

Yellow Ochre and Iron Glaze
Cone 03

Lithium Carbonate.	29 %
Kaolin	14
Silica.	57
	100 %
Add: Red Iron Oxide 10%	
Yellow Ochre.	10 %
Bentonite	2 %

Yoshiro Ikeda achieves a highly decorative effect with low-fire glazes (cone 03 and below) colored with oxides and stains. As an alternative method, after the Crackled White has been fired, he can shorten the multi-step process by brushing on all glazes in layers before doing a single, final firing, although this does not allow the control he desires.

Danville Chadbourne
Indoor/Outdoor Color

by Jim LaVilla Havelin

Several of Danville Chadbourne's sculptures are assembled in his backyard awaiting exhibition.

Danville Chadbourne speaks of the color in his work as painting on clay. He approaches the surfaces of his pieces as a painter would approach a canvas. Interested in the "suggestive and evocative nature of color," Chadbourne notes the influence of non-Western color: tribal weavings from India, Tibet, China and Africa; and of natural color: squash, tomatoes, oranges, red and green chilis.

Confronted with the challenge of the difference between indoor and outdoor sculptures in terms of color and surface, he describes his method for each.

Indoor pieces, safe from the elements, are simply painted. Chadbourne applies acrylic paint to cone 08 bisqueware. The surface is then sanded to remove as much color as he wants and to expose the porous clay. The surface is then stained with acrylic washes. Surfaces acquire a painterly appearance.

For works outdoors, meant to look timeless and aged, subject to bleaching sun, and needing to contrast/complement the surfaces of bronze or concrete, Chadbourne narrows his palette. He applies oxides, body stains or glazes to Cone 08 bisqueware. Then the surface is sponged down to leave as much residue in the porous scratched surface as he wants. Sometimes Chadbourne will apply matt or semi-matt glazes or underglazes to certain areas and then the piece is fired to cone 2.

"Extreme Gravitation—
The Myth of Coinci-
dence," 7 feet in height,
stoneware, with concrete.

"Silent Marker Along the Tortured Path," 8 feet in height, stoneware. Grays, greens and mud browns—earth, grass, rock, storm-sky colors—sit atop a rock-like protruding bottom. The bottom shape, which was inspired by the way some cacti grow, was mirrored by a boulder in the background at Beeville. Six beads stand tall: a nouvelle child's stacking toy, a silent marker. Gunmetal, serpentine, patina, reflects the world around it, even as it asserts a timelessness. And in the surfaces of the stoneware with scrapes and scratches, as well as pigments, glazes and treatments applied, the piece looks like it has always been there—a sentinel, a marker.

"Miracle at the Axis of Desire," 45 inches in height, earthenware, with acrylic and ply-wood.The colors Chad-bourne chooses are non-Western. Chad-bourne collects textiles from around the world and much of his color sense is grounded in Indian, Middle Eastern, African and Australian Aboriginal color schemes and combinations. The colors are saturated for the works indoors, more subtle for outdoor works, which are played upon by sunlight and the elements. Some-times the balances in the colors help to carry the turns and teeters of the structures. It's had to say if what's scratched away is the faddish or con-temporary, or if what's scratched in is picto-graph, fossil, memory, time—a patina, a mark of that passage.

Dust and Wax

by Philippe Faraut

Time has produced the rich, warm patina observed on ancient clay sculptures displayed in museums. The combination of years of dust, cleaning and handling has created surfaces that can look like leather, wood or stone depending on the original color of the earthenware. The clay busts produced centuries ago were sometimes glazed, but most were simply waxed. It was, and remains, the best way to preserve the integrity of details, and provide some degree of protection against dust and stains on unglazed ware. Through application of clay dust and wax, this technique creates the subtle look of ancient patinas without the wait.

Using different colors of clay dust on different clay bodies provides for a wide variety of tones. For example, a red clay sculpture with a light brown dusting of clay looks a little bit like wood, while a brown sculpture with a light white clay dust looks like leather. For a sculpture that would look like limestone (as shown here), I used white, low-fire earthenware clay for both the bust and the pa-

tina. The bust was fired to maturation (Cone 05). As a word of caution, you should always experiment on fired samples before attempting this type of patina on a valued piece, as it takes a little practice to achieve good results. Since this type of patina is somewhat translucent, your sculpture must be built carefully to prevent cracks during drying and firing. Any repairs done after firing might be visible through the wax.

On unglazed works, a wax finish is the best way to preserve the integrity of details, and provide some degree of protection against dust and stains.

Process

Rub four or five damp rags (white cotton t-shirts work best) against a block of wet clay until saturated. Hang in a warm place until rags and clay are bone dry (figure 1).

Spray floor wax* over the entire piece (figure 2). Caution: Work outdoors or in a spray booth.

Immediately after spraying, slap one of the clay-loaded rags against the piece repeatedly until the right amount of dust sticks to the wax (figure 3). A dust mask is required for this step. At first, this step can be unnerving because it sometimes looks blotchy. Add more wax until you are satisfied with the results. When the desired look has been achieved, you need to spray a final layer of wax to obtain a satin finish (figure 4).

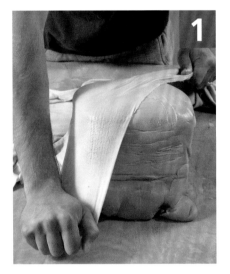
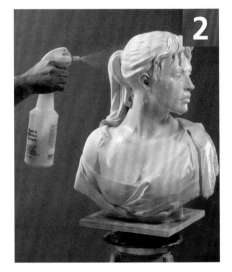
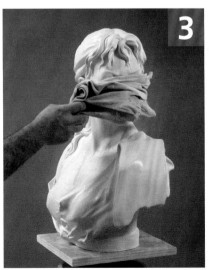

Lundmark All-Wax Floor Wax for asphalt tile, vinyl, linoleum, etc., is available from your local hardware store or it can be ordered online at www.doitbest.com.

Choi Sung-Jae
Expressive Slip Drawings

by Phil Rogers

"Meditation, Journey IV," 19½ inches in diameter, stoneware with white slip.

The indigenous clays of Korea tend to be rich in iron. The often-large, country-made Ongii storage jars, so prized by Korean households, are made from clay of this type. They are decorated with a glaze made from clay mixed with wood ash and a little raw lead. The effect is a rich chestnut brown on dark chocolate. The decoration is often made with fingers through the wet glaze; sweeping, gestural marks to represent a plant or a fish that envelope the form. In the very largest of these jars, the marks show a burst of creative energy that involves the potter's whole body in a dancelike motion. This expressive drawing also required the nonchalant confidence of someone so comfortable with a technique that both hc and the drawing were as one. Glaze and clay caught in a frozen moment of time. A few intense, yet measured, seconds forever recorded for better or for worse.

During the fifteenth and sixteenth centuries, the potters, faced with somber clays, developed decorative techniques that relied upon the use of white slip to lighten the surface of the clay. Four specific techniques were used to coat the pots surface: 1) Pots were impressed, often with complicated repeating patterns and then coated with white slip. Later, when leather hard, the white slip was scraped away to reveal the stamped pattern as an inlay against the surrounding darkness. 2) Pots were dipped in white slip and then painted with iron rich pigment to provide a deep contrast between the lustrous black pattern and the light background. 3) White slip was brushed onto the pot often with coarse brushes, leaving behind a background of great movement that provided the canvas for iron painting as in the pots from the Keryong kilns near Taejon. 4) Potters also would draw through the slip with a sharp point to reveal the dark body beneath. This style of pottery mak-

"Meditation, Autumn IV," 10 inches in height, stoneware with white slip.

proach the technique from a modern viewpoint. These potters are using traditional materials but, by extending their making repertoire and incorporating the influences of nineteenth- and twentieth-century art, both Oriental and occidental, they are making a new statement of strength and vitality. Choi is one such potter.

All pottery begins with form. Form is the potter's language; it is the primary focus of the potter's attention (if it isn't, it should be); the foundation upon which all else is built. Form can sometimes be all that is required; pure and vulnerable, a vehicle for the vagaries of the kiln. Form also can be the skeleton over which we drape a sculpted pattern. It also can provide a canvas. Choi Sung-jae uses form to carry the narrative of his paintings in a very skillful but deceptively simple way. As a Korean, he instinctively understands Asian minimalist composition and uses the proportions of each piece to emphasize distance and space with perfect placement within his three-dimensional frame. The space between the different components of the drawing is as important as the marks themselves. "Meditation, Autumn IV" and "Meditation, Dream III" are fine examples of Choi's organization of space and line. In Meditation, Autumn IV, the bird is on one visible face and the sweeping lines suggesting hanging branches or the tall blades of an Iris spread across two faces. The device of creating an image that incorporates two faces,

ing is known as Punchong, and it is revered among Koreans who are justly proud of a style that is uniquely theirs.

The Korean people—surprisingly, given their nation's less-than-stable history—retain a strong sense of their own identity. The intense pride they have in their ceramics history manifests itself in a desire for many contemporary Korean potters to continue to work in the Punchong tradition. Unfortunately, and all too often, the result is weak, unconvincing pastiche that contributes nothing new. However, there are a small number of younger potters who have embraced Punchong in a new and exciting way, extending and revitalizing a tradition by choosing to ap-

"Meditation, Dream III," 5 inches in height, stoneware with white slip.

thereby breaking the form, extends the frame beyond that which we were expecting and encourages the viewer to see the object fully as a three-dimensional piece. The elongated proportion of Meditation, Dream III provides a panorama. The two birds oppose each other, the space between is self explanatory—it is water—it is not drawn, not even suggested, but we know it is water. Choi hasn't drawn water, yet we feel its wetness. The mallet form of "Meditation, Dawn V," is an illustration of a playful sense of form and proportion, and a move away from narrative drawing to a pure form of abstraction.

Many of Choi's pieces are press molded. He makes the large molds from slab-constructed originals. This technique, although time consuming and physically demanding, allows him to repeat a shape exactly and, in turn, to play with variations in the decoration on the same shapes. He is a fine thrower and, as in Meditation, Dawn V, he displays the nonchalant throwing style of his Punchong forebearers, although the form of this particular piece owes much to the Ongii potters. The plates too are quite remarkable. To design within a circle is not easy. Paintings are square or rectangular not circular—circular is flying in the face of convention. Yet he manages it with

Process

I have watched Choi decorate, and it is a wonder to behold. After coating the leather-hard clay with a liberal thickness of silica rich white slip, he crouches to be at eye level and pauses. The slip must be caught at just the right moment: too wet and it will run; too dry and his finger won't penetrate to the iron rich body beneath. After a few moments of thought and consideration, he explodes into a frenzy of quick, darting movements and the scene appears, as if by magic. Of course he has done this many times before, and the masterful confidence born from experience is obvious. His fingers are his primary tools, but he will make marks with frayed rope, cloth and rounded wooden sticks. His trademark duck is always done with a thumb and thumbnail.

Choi fires his works at a relatively low temperature, for a stoneware potter. There are two advantages in this that help him achieve the effects he desires. One is that the thin walls of the molded pieces remain flat during the firing. At a higher temperature there would be the tendency to warp or slump. Secondly, the contrast between the white slip and the body underneath remains at its most effective.

**"Meditation, Dawn V,"
Punchong vase, 15½ inches
in height, stoneware with
white slip, by Choi Sung-Jae.**

ease. "Meditation, Journey IV" is an example of abstract expressionism at its best, and is truly an evocation of the essence of Korean decorative sensibilities.

Choi's pots have an immense and haunting presence. It was this presence that so captivated me that day in the basement gallery. They are works of importance in a crowded and often mundane ceramics world. They are moments captured in a burst of creative passion; moments with which we are all familiar. They capture those warm and still days on a riverbank, watching the ducks winding their way in and out of the overhanging branches of a willow. They capture the movement of the water, the faint breeze that bends a reed, the gentle bow-shaped wave

a duck makes while moving gracefully through the water. Most of all Choi's works are what every good ceramic work should be—they are a celebration of clay and glaze. There is no pretense, nor fuss. The drawing is spontaneous. Every mark, every nuance is there to be seen, nothing hidden, just as in the Ongii jars. The words I used earlier now seem to bear a familiar resonance: Glaze and clay caught in a frozen moment of time. A few intense, yet measured, seconds forever recorded.

It is probably a cliché but nevertheless true, that Choi's works are imbued with a timeless quality. They are as much of today as any ceramics can be, yet they carry with them a nation's ceramic heritage in contemporary expression.

Mitch Lyons
A Marriage of Ceramics and Printmaking

by Lisa McVey

New London, Pennsylvania, artist Mitch Lyons brushes colored clay slip onto his 25-year-old slab of clay in preparation for pulling a monoprint. The slab, which started out as a ¼-inch layer of rolled white stoneware, is now roughly 2 inches thick.

As the mid-morning light streams in through the wall of windows behind him, clay monoprint artist Mitch Lyons leans forward to trail a swirl of colored slip onto a leather-hard clay slab.

He pauses to glance over his work surface, which is strewn with a dozen rudimentary tools. He selects a small hand-cut stencil and lays it on the slab. Next, he grabs a chunk of pastel, made by pouring colored slip onto plain newsprint and leaving it to dry overnight.

Outside, a flock of blackbirds swoop in over the gently rolling hills. They land nearby, flapping their wings and squawking loudly. Lyons is oblivious. He is at once distanced, yet inextricably engrossed in his work.

He proceeds to finely grate the colored pastel over the stencil, then gently lifts it. Left behind is an image reminiscent of a leaping dancer's silhouette. He follows with a light misting of water from a spray bottle to turn the dusting of pastel into slip again.

Similar scenes of Lyons manipulating his plate surface have played out thousands of times in his garage-turned-studio, located in historic New London, Pennsylvania. This past year, he celebrated a silver anniversary of sorts: a milestone in time using his studio slab, and looking back 25 years to when he first began making clay monoprints in earnest after successfully marrying two art forms.

Discovering a New Medium

Lyons discovered the clay monoprint process almost serendipitously. One day, after rolling out and pulling up a slab to build a three-dimensional vessel, he noticed color from the oxides left behind on the white canvas underneath the slab. "That was the first hint that there was a possibility of printing with clay," he said.

As a grad student, Lyons pulled his first true clay print. But, he says, it took twelve more years and a lot of experimentation before he felt he had a "genuine idea" for a new medium. In 1980, Lyons assembled a 6-foot by 6-foot permanent clay slab in his studio to be used as his plate surface. He added a 4-foot extension in 1995.

The process of making a print begins by applying colored slip onto the slab. When it dries, the colored clay is inlaid in the slab using a rolling pin. Lyons also uses ceramic techniques such as slip trailing, stamping and incising to infuse texture and color into the plate surface.

When Lyons first began making clay monoprints, he added food coloring to inorganic colorant, like iron oxide, to make colored slip. He later used permanent organic pigments that painters use, like Ultramarine Blue, along with inorganic pigments that potters use, like Cerulean Blue Stain. This allowed Lyons to make a print, pull up the slab, make a vessel and fire it. The organic pigments burned out, leaving the ceramic stains to make the fired colors.

He now makes slip by mixing china clay and water using a kitchen blender. He adds a few drops of sodium silicate as a drying agent. He mixes organic pigments into the kaolin slip.

Lyons' studio slab was a quarter-inch think layer of rolled white stoneware clay when he first began using it. Now, the plate surface is roughly two inches thick—a swirl of colors and layers of clay that have accumulated during 25 years of printmaking.

Lyons originally used rice paper to make prints, and later found several watercolor papers that worked well. In the 1970s, researchers from DuPont, the Delaware–based chemical company, gave Lyons a few samples of a non-woven, spun-bonded fiber material called Reemay.

The samples sat in a drawer for a few months before he decided to try them. "I thought I needed an absorbent material," he said. "But, this non-absorbent surface worked great. It worked better than paper."

The Reemay has an electrostatic charge which bonds with the negatively charged clay. A company in Old Hickory, Tennessee, now manufactures the material.

Process

The process of making a clay monoprint is like a woodcut, etching, lithograph and monoprint all rolled into one, according to Lyons. The deep marks he makes are like those in woodcuts or etching. Before he prints, Lyons places plain newsprint over the slab and rolls it flat. The texture is brought back to the surface like a lithograph, he explained.

Once he is satisfied with the layers, color and texture he has created, he masks off the area to be printed. Next, he lightly sprays the substrate and slab with water. The slip softens slightly. He places the Reemay over the slab and rolls again, making a print from the planographic surface.

Paper merely pulled the color. The Reemay pulls off a thin layer of clay slip. Lyons' clay monoprints are saturated with color that has layers of intensity. "Since I have an affinity with the material, I wanted to pull the clay off and not just the color," said Lyons. "It's a perfect marriage for me."

Finding Harmony and Balance

Lyons releases himself from rigid rules and strict formulas when making a print. "Unlearning what you've learned," is how he puts it. "It's more about getting out of your own way. If I try to control it and structure it and come in with a strong preconception, it doesn't work for me," said

Two vessels, 15 inches in height, handbuilt (on wheel) porcelain, with inlaid porcelain slips, reduction fired.

Clay Monoprinting

by Mitch Lyons

A slab of stoneware clay is first rolled out about ¼ inch thick onto a piece of plywood. China clay and water are mixed together to form a slip. Both organic pigments such as Rose Madder, and inorganic pigments such as yellow ochre are mixed into the wet slip for color. This colored slip is applied to the leather-hard slab, dried and rolled into the slab with a rolling pin. Colored slips are added to the slab using various ceramic techniques such as slip trailing, stenciling, stamping, etc. Once the slab is dry, a damp substrate is placed over the "plate" and rolled with a rolling pin. This pressure pulls a thin layer of clay from the plate. More than one monoprint can be pulled. My clay slab was rolled out in 1980 and has thousands of colored slips on the surface.

Lyons. "It's not only about artistic talent. It's about becoming involved, but relaxed and liberated."

Bill Daly, a lifelong mentor to Lyons, says "Clay people see him as a printmaker, and the press and paper artists see him as a ceramics artist. On the one hand, it's a strange location to be in. On the other hand," he mused, "it isn't so far flung. There is a two-dimensional connection between storytelling and printmaking and the three-dimensional process of making a ceramic vessel. There is a connection, and Mitch found it and used it for a lifetime."

Marriage Going Strong

Lyons considers himself a ceramics artist who makes prints. His vessels and prints are born of slabs, he said. Bea, his wife, sees it differently. "She says, 'Mitch, you're in denial. You are a printmaker,'" recounts Lyons.

Lyons does have a slight nagging sense he's between two genres. And while some skeptics still don't accept the art form, Lyons remains undeterred. It comes with the territory for a man who discovered a new medium more than 35 years ago, has worked decades to perfect it, and is still open to new possibilities.

Inset left: Lyons pulls a piece of Reemay off of his slab and checks the transfer image.

Detail of "Eutectic," 43 inches in height, clay monoprint.

Printing and Embossing with Linocuts

by Paul Andrew Wandless

Block or relief printing is a great transfer technique for any kind of image, text or design you want on your work. Whether simple or complex, finished linocuts can even be the finished works on their own (figure 1). When inked with underglaze or slips, you can use the blocks to print directly onto clay or push them into the surface for embossing. Linoleum or lino, as it's commonly called, is flexible and works on flat and curved surfaces making it versatile to use. Clay, plaster, wood and rubber can also be used for block printing.

Creating your linocut

Lino has a smooth gray or brown surface with a backing made of a coarse fabric called hessian that helps reduce cracking. Using a fine grit sand paper, remove any oils, scratches or imperfections on the surface before carving. This also makes for a more receptive surface to ink up with underglaze or slip. You can soften the surface of old or stiff sheets of lino by lightly ironing the surface or by holding a blow dryer or heat gun 6–12 inches from the back. Move the heat source in a circular pattern or from side to side and don't sit still on one area too long. You only need to do this for a few minutes and the lino will be soft as butter for carving.

Block printing reverses the image so you'll need to carve your designs backwards so they will print correctly on the clay. You can use tracing paper or carbon paper to reverse the original image onto your block before carving (figure 2). This is especially important if using text or numbers.

Carve on a tabletop and use a bench hook or C-clamp to hold your lino in place. A bench hook can be picked up wherever you buy your carving tools for the lino. Traditional or standard lino/wood gouges (figure 3) are used for carving the surface and can be found in any craft or art store. Never carve with your hand in the path of the gouge and never hold the block on your lap when carving. Gouges are extremely sharp so be very careful when using them.

Assorted linocuts.

Pencil drawing on lino.

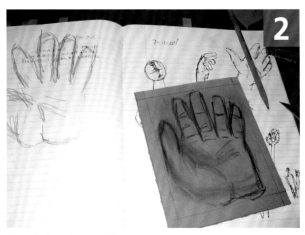

Gouges, lino block, bench hook and sandpaper.

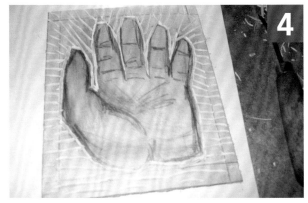

Half-carved lino on bench hook.

Once the reversed image is drawn onto the lino, carve away all the areas you don't want to print with color. The remaining raised areas create the relief image that you'll print or emboss on the clay. Often I use an image where the orientation is important (figure 4).

Printing and Embossing

To print the linocut you'll need a clean, smooth surface, a brayer (small hand roller) and an underglaze or slip that is thick and sticky (figure 5). Having the proper consistency to this ceramic ink is key to the success of the image being transferred cleanly. Commercial underglaze is usually too thin right out of the container, so pour what you need into a small plastic container and let it sit out overnight. Once it's the thickness of yogurt, add clear acrylic printing medium to give it the body and stickiness needed for printing (figure 6). Shoot for a consistency of honey for the best printing results. An easy option is to purchase a semimoist commercial underglaze that's ready to use right out of the tube and formulated specifically for printing purposes.

Back: semimoist underglazes, GDC Velvet underglaze, acrylic transparent base printing medium, small container and mixing spoon. Front: clay slab, linocut with baren above it, rubber roller on sheet of Plexiglas.

Stirring the acrylic transparent base printing medium and underglaze to produce a ceramic ink of the proper consistency.

Mixing color to make sure consistency is even.

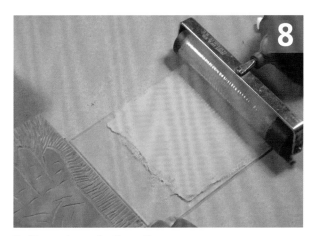

Rolling color onto the roller.

I use Amaco semimoist underglaze in the ¼-ounce tubes for small blocks or single prints, but for larger blocks or multiple prints I thicken the Amaco Velvet, GDC or LUG colors in whatever custom amounts I need. With some practice, though, the underglazes can be applied without being thickened or adding any printing medium. Artist Kathy King prints her linocuts on clay using Amaco LUG Black right out of the bottle with great success and good image clarity. Once you develop a touch for working with a thinner consistency it's just as effective as using the semimoist colors.

Before printing, make sure everything is laid out and ready to go. Prepare extra slabs so you can do all your printing at once and not have to stop and roll out more if you're unhappy with some prints you're getting. For good printing results, the

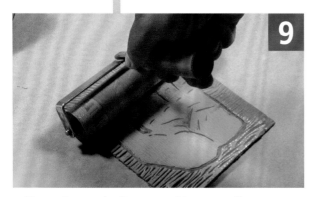

Rolling color on the linocut making sure all areas are covered with color.

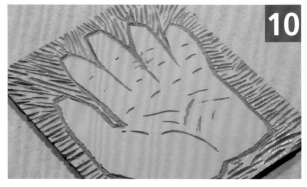

Colored lino with a little shine (indicates the ink is wet and will transfer well).

Placing inked-up block face down.

Rubbing the block with your hands or a baren.

surface of the clay slabs can be somewhat damp, but not sticky or even in the early stages of leather hard.

Put enough ceramic ink for one print on the Plexiglas and mix it with a stick or a spoon to ensure it's even (figure 7). Move the roller back and forth over the color until you have an even coat on the roller (figure 8). Apply an even coat on the linocut making sure all areas are covered with color (figure 9). The ceramic ink should appear wet on the surface of the block when properly covered (figure 10).

Turn the block face down onto the clay slab (figure 11) and gently rub the back of it in a circular motion with your hand or a baren (figure 12) to help transfer the color. Don't wait too long to print the block after it's been inked or the color starts to dry and won't transfer as cleanly. Peel the block off slowly from the clay and see how it came out (figure 13).

The first print will help you answer three questions. Was the ceramic ink mixed to the right consistency, was enough ceramic ink used on the block for good color results and was there enough pressure used for a clean transfer. Many times this first print isn't usable and is considered a test print for this important

Revealing the print.

Top left: Linocut. Top right: In this print, there was uneven pressure and the ceramic ink was too dry when printed. Bottom left: Shows results of good pressure and color.
Bottom right: Shows results of bad pressure on edges; also, ceramic ink was still not wet enough when printed.

What a Relief

A linocut can also be used as if it were a large stamp to emboss a soft clay surface (see photo below). Many artists make custom relief tiles in this fashion. The areas that would normally receive the ceramic ink are now embossed into the clay. Place your linocut face down on a soft piece of clay and rub the back in a circular motion. Don't press so hard that the lino gets stuck. Peel back and the embossing is complete.

You can also add color in the embossed image to make the design appear as a color inlay. Bisque fire the embossing, then apply glaze, underglaze, or stain in the embossed areas with a brush or other applicator and let it dry. Use a damp cloth or sponge to wipe the color off the high areas leaving color only the embossed area.

information (figure 14). Make the necessary adjustments after seeing the test print, if any, and then continue printing the rest of your slabs.

After the Print

Once printed, the clay slabs can be used for whatever handbuilding purposes you want or can even be the finished piece if you like. You can also print on a clay piece that's already built but still in the green stage. This is where your own creativity comes into play based on your work and how best to incorporate the lino image. Thoroughly clean all tools used for the printing process with water.

You may not be a printmaker when you start this process, but you will be an official "Clay Printer" once you've block printed on clay. You just need a curiosity of material and an image to repeat.

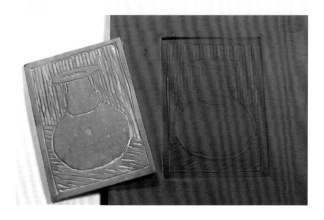

Using Stencils for Multi-Color Decoration

by Paul Andrew Wandless

Stenciling is one of the oldest and simplest techniques for creating single- and multi-color images or designs. Almost any thin sheet of stiff plastic material, such as commercial stencil film, transparencies or acetate, can be used for stencils, making this an easy and convenient method to use in your studio. Stencils are easily cut with an X-Acto knife or heat wand, and the significant advantages of using plastic stencils are that they're easy to clean with water, very durable and last for many years.

Getting Started

Creating a multi-color image using a multi-part stencil is easy to do and it can make a basic design visually more dynamic. The biggest challenge with this technique is deciding how to cut your stencils to separate the colors when creating the different stencil layers. This takes planning, but just remember that the colors will be applied in separate layers and each layer represents a stencil.

I used a stencil heat wand and commercial stencil film (available from art and craft stores) to make three stencils for a five-color image of St. Pablo the Fighter. Since you can apply more than one color on a stencil, two of my stencils will be used for two different colors. This helps maximize color opportunities for a design.

I approach cutting out my stencil images in reverse order. The outline of the image and boxing gloves are cut out of one stencil first, the head and robe are cut out of the second stencil, and the halo is the third stencil (see image at right). While this kind of image can be lined up by eye,

 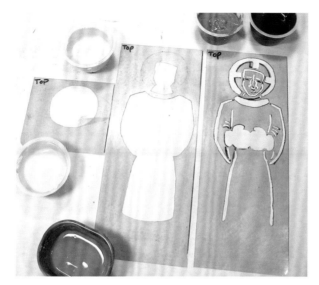

St. Pablo the Fighter was created from a slab decorated using 3 stencils and 5 colors.

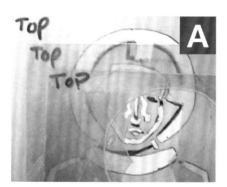 

After you cut your stencils, mark the top left corner of each stencil (left). Line them up in the top left corner to be certain the registration is correct (right).

I make sure all three stencils line up in the top left corner when stacked on each other to ensure proper registration (figures A and B).

Any firing temperature is fine for this process as long as the cone range of the slip or glaze is compatible with the cone range of the clay body you're stenciling the image onto. Colored slips and commercial underglazes can be used on greenware, or you can even use the stencils with glaze on bisqueware.

For best results, the slips or glazes should be a yogurt consistency so the color doesn't bleed underneath the edges of the stencil, blurring your design (unless, of course, that's the effect you're going for). I tend to like the looser edges for my work, but you can also be very neat and precise if that's what your work calls for. Thin slips and underglazes can be thickened by pouring the amount you need into a small tray or pan and letting them sit and stiffen.

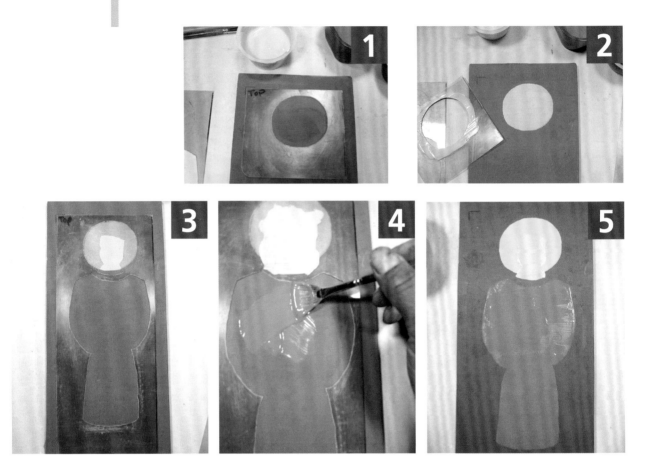

The Stencil Process

Roll out, cut, smooth and mark all the clay slabs you're going to need for your project in advance. In this case, I'm making a total of five images with this multi-colored design. Once the slabs are ready, place all your colored underglazes and brushes within easy reach. Next, mark the clay slab or slabs where the top left corner of the stencils should line up to ensure proper registration.

Layer 1

After lining up the top left corner of the first stencil, lightly rub the stencil to ensure a good seal with the clay surface (fig.1). Brush on an even coat of yellow underglaze for the halo, then immediately peel off the stencil (figure 2). You'll have to wait 5 to 10 minutes or until the shine on the slip has gone dull before using the next stencil. If you don't wait until the color dries to the touch, it will smear when the next stencil is placed over it. Clean the stencil with water and dry it with a paper towel or cloth after each use. Since I'm making five tiles, I'll repeat brushing this first stencil on the remaining four prepared slabs and by the time I'm done, the first slab should be dry and ready for the second stencil.

Layer 2

The second stencil is for two colors and they are both applied at the same time. I register the top left corner of the stencil, but can also plainly see how the stenciled halo matches up with the head (figure 3). Once in place, the first color is brushed on for the head, then the second color for the robe. For large areas like the robe, I work from the inside out to get cleaner edges (figure 4). After applying both colors, I peel back the stencil and let it dry (figure 5).

Layer 3

Once the robe and head have dried to the touch, I register the final stencil, and all of my parts should line up pretty well. As mentioned earlier, I cut my stencils to give myself a little overlap so there will be a little wiggle room on some of the edges. I brush on the red underglaze for the gloves first (figure 6), then brush the black outline on last (figure 7).

The smaller lines cut into the face always smudge a bit with this sten-cil, but I like the look of it since it's on a fighter and works visually with that theme (figure 8). Once all the slabs are stenciled, I'll let the final colors dry and decide what to do with them.

Final Thoughts

See how easy it is to make a five-color stenciled image? I'll treat these slabs as an edition of five prints (images) of St. Pablo the Fighter. I normally frame an edition of images like this or sometimes I'll use them for handbuilding purposes as part of a sculptural work. Several images can be printed on just one large slab as well or you can make one image that can be used in a slump mold to make a plate or platter. You can alter and do more work to these leather-hard slabs, or after bisque firing you can glaze and add more color to them. Once the stencils are made, you'll be surprised at all the uses you can come up with for your image or design.

Relief Printing with Photosensitive Polymer Plates

by Paul Andrew Wandless

Ink a light-engraved block with a contrasting slip to transfer images onto a prepared surface.

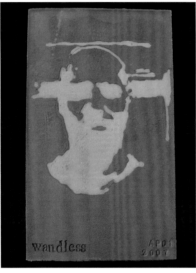

Fill the impression with a contrasting slip and scrape the surface similar to a mishima technique.

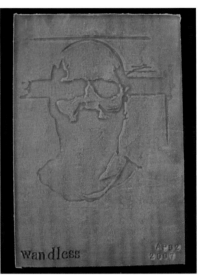

Brush oxides or colorants onto the surface and wipe away the excess, leaving highlights.

Block printing with linocuts, woodcuts and claycuts are three common relief techniques used for image transfer on clay. Printing with photosensitive polymer plates is another relief block technique you can add to this list. The attractive benefit of this technique is that carving isn't necessary to create the image. You just sit back and let the sun do the carving for you. All you need is a transparency with an opaque black negative of an image to be printed and some cool tap water to dissolve away the areas you don't want printed. Another great benefit is that any image can be used, including photographs. This really opens up your design options since you're not limited to only what can be carved by hand with a gouge.

The plates themselves consist of a thin layer of water-soluble, photosensitive polymer on a thin, flexible metal backing. Polymer plates come in light-protected packages and must remain inside until you're ready to expose them to UV light and create your image. Plates come in a variety of sizes from 5×7 inches up to 16×20 inches and are an amber color. They can easily be cut to any custom size you want using a paper cutter, tin snips or heavy-duty scissors. Polymer plates with polyester backing are also available, and are even more flexible than the metal-backed plates.

The process of creating an image with a polymer plate using sunlight is fairly simple and requires no special studio equipment. A transparency with an opaque black negative image is placed on top of a photosensitive polymer plate, held in place with a glass plate of similar dimensions and then exposed to ultraviolet (UV) light from the sun. Where the light hits the surface of the plate, the emulsion hardens; where the light is blocked, the emulsion remains soft. Since the emulsion is water soluble, the unhardened portions can be rinsed away later with cool tap water. These low areas won't be part of the printed image. After exposing the plate for 2–3 minutes to direct sunlight it's rinsed and developed in cool water for 5–10 minutes, creating the relief. The relief plate is exposed to UV light from the sun for an additional 15–30 minutes to harden the remaining emulsion and set the plate. The rehardened plate is then ready to use for relief block printing or embossing. You may find your biggest challenge with the process is deciding which images to use and getting a nice sunny day to expose the plate.

Making a Black-and-White Negative Transparency

There are several options for making a transparency to use with polymer plates. Copiers, printers and computers work great with photos and already existing images, but you can also elect to draw directly on a transparency with a black marker for a freehand image. Here are three important things to remember:

1. The image must be black and white, or converted to black and white for best contrast when copying on the transparency.

2. Light hardens the polymer so the printed areas need to be clear in your transparency. This means you need to make a negative of your image on the transparency so the printing areas are clear and the nonprinting areas are opaque black. (Note: the white areas on the original black-and-white image on paper will be the clear areas on your transparency.) You will also need two transparencies of your image so you can sandwich them together to ensure an opaque black. One transparency is not dark enough to completely block out the light. Depending on the quality of ink of the machine being used, you may even need to sandwich three transparencies to achieve an opaque black (figure 2).

3. Since this is a relief block technique, the image will be reversed during the printing process. This means that once you decide on the final image it will need to be reversed if the orientation is important or if you're using text.

Create an Image: Photocopiers and Printers

So how do you actually go about making your image once you've chosen what you want to burn into the polymer plate? If you're going to use a ready-made image or photograph, then a photocopier or printer is a fairly simple solution. Most copiers and printers have options or features to convert a positive image into a negative image and to change the size or dimensions. All machines have a black-and-white mode available for printing and copying. (Caution: Be sure to use the correct transparency sheets for your printer or copier as indicated in its owner manual. Using incompatible sheets could ruin your machine.)

If you don't own a machine that has these options, just take your ready-made image or photograph to the nearest copy shop and they can do all of this for just a few dollars. Just say you need two copies of a black-and-white negative on a transparency of the image you're providing. To reverse your image once it's printed on the transparency, just flip it over before placing it onto the polymer plate.

Create an Image: Computers and Digital Manipulation

Another way to create an image is using a computer, scanner, digital camera and an image manipulation program. These digital options give you the freedom to change, adjust and alter an image to your own custom needs. I set my HP PCS 2200 series All-In-One Scanner/Printer to black-and-white mode and scanned a photo of myself. I also used my digital camera to take some photos of my hand. I imported these images into my laptop and used Photoshop to do all of my image manipulation.

Prepare an Image

I begin with opening potential image files (figure 1) and start getting them ready for copying onto a transparency. Since I'll be using 5×7-inch polymer plates, I'll need to adjust the images to fit those parameters. I use Adobe Photoshop for both resizing images and making negatives for the copy shop.

To make the scanned black-and-white self-portrait smaller, I select the Image dropdown menu, select Image Size, and adjust the width to 5 inches with a 300 dpi resolution (figure 2). I need two images so I create a new file (canvas) that is 8½×11 inches with a 300 dpi resolution and the background contents set on transparent. I cut and paste the images side by side to create a two-up image of the positive. This image needs to be converted to a negative, so select Adjustments and then Invert (figure 3). Now my image is ready to print onto paper and take to the copy shop to be copied onto a transparency (figure 4).

Prepare a Transparency

With the image on paper (figure 5, right) now copied onto a transparency (figure 5, left) at a local copy shop, I'm ready to make my transparency sandwich. I have a 5×7 inch sheet of glass that I place on my transparency to keep it in full contact with the plate, and I also use it as a template for cutting the transparency with a razor blade knife (figure 6). A ruler, cutting board and painter's tape are the other items used for this

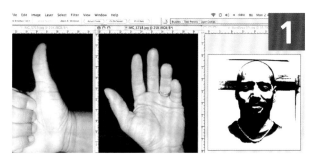

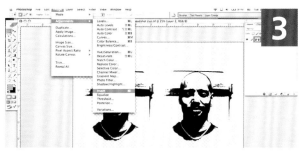

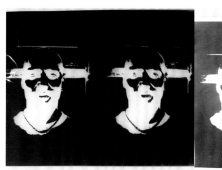

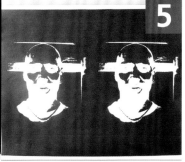

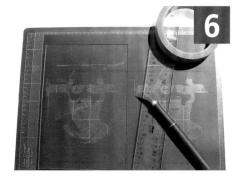

step. After cutting the transparency, place one image on top of the other and visually line them up, them secure them together with painter's tape. Hold it up to the sky and make sure the black is opaque and no light comes through (figure 7). If light passes through, add a third transparency to darken it more.

Exposing the Plate

On the day I'm going to expose the photosensitive polymer plate there are some clouds passing by, but it's mid-day, the summer sun is bright and I only need 2 to 4 minutes of bright, consistent sun for exposing the plate. If you don't have a bright sunny day, it's best to wait until you do for best results. All that's needed other than bright sunlight is a timer, polymer plates, an opaque negative and the glass plate to hold it down (figure 8). You should be in close proximity to a sink, as well, so you can rinse the plate off when exposure is finished.

Now it's time to start the exposing session. Remove the 5×7 polymer plate from the protective package with the metal side down

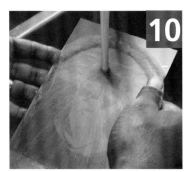

and the amber (polymer) side up. Immediately place the negative on the amber polymer surface and place the sheet of glass on top (figure 9). The glass keeps the negative firmly in place and in full contact with the plate. Note: I didn't reverse (flop) the negative in this demo, because I'm not concerned about the orientation of the image when printed. If you're using text or the orientation does matter, make sure you flop the image to ensure that it prints correctly (reversed).

After exposing the plate to the sun for two minutes, remove the glass and negative, and take the polymer plate inside to rinse and develop it in cool tap water (figure 10). Allow the cool water to run over the entire image and the unexposed, water-sol-

uble polymer should start to soften and wash away. Once this starts to happen, soak it in a shallow pan of cool water and watch the polymer melt away. The gold color starting to appear is the metal backing and the dark amber is the raised, UV-hardened image. After about ten minutes, run cool water over the plate again and use a soft nylon brush to help clean off the soft polymer (figure 11).

Soaking the plate in water makes even the hardened areas feel a bit tacky, so once all the unexposed areas are rinsed, take the plate back outdoors into the sun for up to 30 minutes to re-harden the emulsion. Placing it in the sun hardens all areas of the plate and dries it off as well. Once you can touch the plate and it's no longer wet or tacky in any

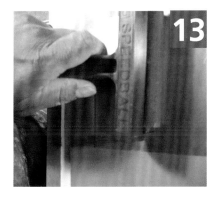

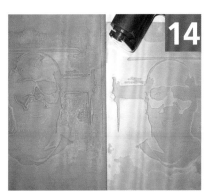

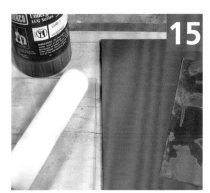

area you're ready to print. Placing the plate and negative side-by-side shows how well the plate picks up all the detail and how effective this method is for creating a photographic relief (figure 12). The ragged, light amber color around the edges of the plate are thin areas of polymer that didn't completely wash off creating a very thin film. A longer soaking in water or more brushing would have taken all of this off the plate. I don't mind having a little "noise" in my print so I leave some polymer behind. I tend to trim all my linocuts to follow the contour of my image and this can be done to the polymer plate

as well. Use tin snips to cut the plate in any shape you want.

See how fast this process can be and how few items are needed? Once you have your negatives made it only takes about 30–45 minutes to complete the whole process of exposing, developing and rehardening the plate. I enjoy being outdoors and making the plates using the sun, but you can also do this process indoors using a UV lamp to expose the polymer plates as well. The timing is a little different so you'll need to do small test plates to get the right exposure time for the UV lamp wattage you are using.

Printing with the Plates

Use the hardened plates to imprint the clay surface or as a relief block. To imprint, use your hand or a roller to press the plate into a soft clay surface (figure 13). Gently pull the plate back to reveal a wonderful photographic impression (figure 14). Use the clay slab for any hand-building process. The plate can also be used to imprint plates or platters. Another approach is to use the mishima technique of inlaying color inside the impression. I use colored Amaco Velvet underglaze or my own colored slips for mishima on greenware. You can also bisque first then use glaze in the impressed areas.

The polymer plates also print nicely as relief blocks. Use commercial underglaze and a foam roller to apply the color (figure 15). I use Amaco LUG series underglaze for all my relief printing with a regular foam roller found in the painting section of any hardware store. Load up the foam roller with underglaze, completely cover the plate with color, then print onto the clay surface (figure 16). Use your hand or a printmaking baren to gently rub the back in a circular motion to transfer the color from the plate to the clay. The image here shows some of the "noise" around the edges that I enjoy visually in my work (figure 17). If you like a cleaner look, trim the plate or simply wipe away unwanted color from the clay surface.

Creating a photographic relief without all the carving by hand is a great project to try. Have fun with polymer plates and the printing processes associated with them and see how it opens up your work visually.

Photosensitive Polymer Plates

I used polymer plates acquired from McClain's Printmaking Supplies (www.imcclains.com) for this article. McClain's is a printmaking supply company specializing in relief printing supplies. They sell the polymer plates under the name of Solar Plates (item # D1900) in 3 different sizes and all have metal backing. There are other suppliers of the product as well and a quick search on the internet will guide you to a source that is right for your needs.

Majolica Madness

by David Gamble

"Karen" and "Bob," 14 inches in height, earthenware with commercial glazes. Treating the clay surface as a canvas and exploring the effects of layering glazes opens up a world of surface possibilities. For painters who work in clay, commercial glazes provide a great palette of color and texture.

After presenting hundreds of workshops through the years to art teachers and potters, using a wide variety of commercial glazes, I've discovered that their enthusiasm about glazing possibilities is overwhelmed by the vast extent of what's available. There are just so many products that it's hard to know where to start and what to purchase without spending a fortune. Of the many possible glazing methods and techniques, majolica is one of the most popular and offers such a rich variety of possibilities.

From Then to Now

Traditional majolica is simply earthenware that has a lead-based glaze made opaque white with the addition of tin oxide, which is then decorated with wide palette of colors. It was named majolica because it came out of the port of Majorca off the coast of Spain. Variations of the technique took on the names of their sources—faience from Faenza, Italy and delft from Delft, Holland—each with the same idea but different design elements. Starting in the fifteenth century, the technique spread to different countries, each adding different decorative elements to what was done previously. Thus, we have a variety of different names and looks to this tin-glazed earthenware.

Most contemporary clay forms, decorations and firing methods are not really new but are just a twist on or combination of something done in

Begin with a glossy base coat of a color of your choice.

Apply three coats to ensure good coverage.

Apply three coats of low-fire white—glossy, matt or a mix.

The base coat will break up through the white surface.

the past. I consider myself a painter that happens to work in clay, and am constantly looking for techniques to create interesting surfaces on a low-fire clay body in an (electric) oxidation firing.

The majolica technique of glazing seemed to be more akin to working like a painter, and I found the majolica process, and the wide assortment of commercial glazes available, to be the best way for me to do the detailed work I wanted. Prime the "canvas" with a white base glaze.

Paint an image on top. The glaze melts together when fired. This all seemed familiar. Okay, if I'm going to work like a painter, what about my paints? Painters haven't mixed their own colors for a few centuries and tubes and jars of paint are available everywhere. I had worked in the ceramics industry for three decades and had learned that there are thousands of different glazes available. I should be able to paint pieces with great depth with the glazes that were available commercially.

Use a regular pencil to roughly sketch on the dried glaze.

Block in colors using majolica-type glazes.

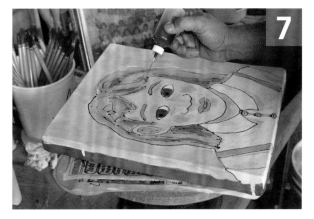

Fire to cone 04 then touch up areas and add accents.

The Twist

The concept for a series of work never follows any certain path for me. In my current work, I began with an idea to recreate a sketchbook drawing on clay. That turned into 11×14-inch wet slabs to which I attached sides to make them stick out from the wall when hung—something like a stretched canvas rather than just a hanging tile. This size and shape gave me a flat clay surface that was the approximate size of a sheet of sketchbook paper and could be recognized as that. From that point on, living got in the way of the original idea. By the time the first group was ready to bisque, I'd made other slabs the same size and transferred images from manhole covers to these same shapes, then produced two more series of images. After making more than 100 pieces, I still had not created a sketch-type drawing, but that's the way it all works. One idea leads to the next.

While searching through old photos looking for something else, I came across my old kindergarten class photo. Wow! I hadn't seen this photo in decades and seeing all my old friends and classmates brought back a lot of great memories of school and the neighborhood. I immediately took the class portrait to my studio and set it up. By the next day I had three pieces glazed in a somewhat majolica-technique and ready to fire. I wanted the images to be as loose as I could make them

"Cheryl," 14 inches in height. Layering glazes and multiple firings can result in unusual effects in both color and surface. Explore using different base glazes layered with both light and heavy applications of glazes and stains on top.

"Ted," 14 inches in height. The cracked white background results from adding a thick coat of the background glaze after the first firing so that it will pull apart the glaze underneath.

without distorting them too much. I had used a familiar terra cotta clay that would allow me to fire these pieces a number of times.

The first firing for me is a way to lay things out. I start with laying down base coats, but instead of a traditional low-fire majolica white I use various cone 05 low-fire glazes as the base and pile on the layers. For example, I start with three coats of a glossy color, which could be black, blue, key lime, etc. (figures 1 and 2). Then I put another three coats of a low-fire white commercial glaze, sometimes matt, sometimes glossy, sometimes a mix (figures 3 and 4). The idea is to have the color of the

bottom glaze break up through the white. Once all these base glazes are down and dry, I create the image by first sketching it very roughly in with a regular pencil that will burn out (figure 5).

Next, I block in the colors (figure 6) using majolica glazes from several different glaze manufacturers so that I have a wide range of color to choose from. They all seem fairly compatible when I fire them to cone 04, and if you add them all up, there are well over 400, though some are very close in color. That's a huge palette and they can be mixed to create even more hues to fit your projects.

Once the piece has been glazed fired to cone 04, I touch up areas, places I want to bring out more or recede—adding more of the same or a different color to a specific area (figure 7).

I sometimes pile a background glaze on thick on a second firing so that it will pull apart and the glaze underneath will show back through. To me that's when it becomes an interesting surface. This helps create depth within the image and pulls your eye into the surface. While some would consider these glaze defects, I'm actively trying to create them with some control. Yes, when clay is treated like a canvas, it allows me to think about painting and paint about thinking.

Bridget Chérie Harper
Visual Diaries

by Paul Lewing

Sometimes you just have to have an octopus, or a violin, or maybe a fig tree. If your work is about both painting and form, as Bridget Chérie Harper's is, you need a model. Harper's china-painted porcelain sculpture, "Natural Selection," features an octopus sensuously wrapping around a female torso to reach a ripe fig, so she bought a whole octopus and took pictures of fig trees.

Despite majoring in art in college, Harper resisted the path of an artist, hoping for a more stable career. Her mother, a talented professional artist, taught her how to see, but provided an example of the difficulties of raising children on an artist's income. When she was sixteen, she came to Arizona from Tennessee for an exhibition of her mother's work. The desert landscape intrigued Harper, and she decided to attend Arizona State University, where she initially majored in business. She met Kurt Weiser, who became her mentor and ally. Weiser even arranged an internship for her in a pottery in Thailand.

Harper worked as a detail artist on a team creating sculptures for cruise ships, and served as a consultant for a public art memorial to Frank Lloyd Wright. These jobs were her introduction to figurative sculpture. Since the late 90s she has been building a ceramics program at Tempe's Cutural Services and teaching evening ceramics classes.

A few years ago she did not intend to be either a figurative sculptor or a china painter. She had been throwing and carving porcelain forms since her student days, but felt she needed a new path. Her admiration for classical sculpture led her to the idea of the torso with missing appendages, but this confronted her with the dilemma of what to do with the surface. At this point, she recalled a basket filled with vials of china paint that she'd bought for fifty cents at an antique mall years before. She was familiar with china paint from

The front of the finished sculpture, "Natural Selection," 20 inches in height.

Harper begins the painting process on the front of the sculpture.

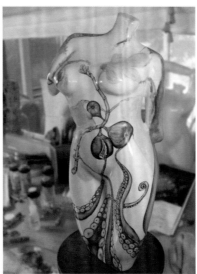

After an initial firing to cones 019–017, she begins to lay the figs and leaves behind the central image.

The front of the finished sculpture, "Natural Selection," 20 inches in height.

Weiser's vessel forms, and her work progressed very quickly from that point. She never had any lessons in china painting. She just picked up a brush and began painting. China paint provided the perfect medium for her realistic and evocative imagery in rich, lush colors.

"The porcelain figure became a canvas and the surface a visual diary," Harper says. "My surrealistic paintings on the classical forms are a byproduct of my life. They come from dreams, relationships and everyday encounters." In the past, Harper kept written diaries, but since the inception of these pieces, although she may make notes in her sketchbook, sculpture has taken their place in her life.

Each piece begins as a handbuilt form, from which she makes a mold. Slip-cast forms survive multiple chi-

na-paint firings better than handbuilt ones, and the mold allows her to produce both a consistent series and replacements for pieces lost along the way. Harper usually casts two or three pieces from each mold. She bisques her figures to cone 9, buried up to the waist in sand to prevent slumping. She then sprays on a coat of clear glaze, and fires the piece to cone 5.

She gathers her imagery sources, sketches a bit, and begins painting, moving around the figure. The challenge is to wrap the imagery around the form in a spontaneous and effective way. "When people look at my pieces, I want them to notice the elegance of the sculptural form and the complex relationship between the form and the painting," Harper explains. "The challenge is to make it look believable." The painting may take several weeks, and the work will be fired three or four times to a temperature range of cone 019–017.

Harper likes to complete as much of the painting in a single firing as she can, but often deepens colors and adds highlights in later firings. She tends to apply the paint heavily at first, in broad impressionistic strokes, then blend colors on the piece. For this, she mixes her colors with a traditional "open" (non-drying) oil-based medium.

Bridget Chérie Harper sees her work as both painting and sculpture, bound together by ceramics. She has had to conquer all the problems of handbuilding, slipcasting, glazing and china painting. While her china painting materials are very traditional, her integration of form and decoration is not. Whether it's an image as sinuous as an octopus or as geometric as a violin, the painting wraps around the torso in perfect harmony with the form.

Getting Started

After modeling a satisfactory figure, Harper makes a mold and casts it in porcelain. She has found that slip-cast figures survive multiple china-paint firings better than handbuilt forms. This also allows her to produce works in series. She bisque fires the figures to cone 9, buried up to the waist in sand to prevent slumping. She then sprays on a coat of clear glaze and fires the pieces to cone 5. Then the real work begins.

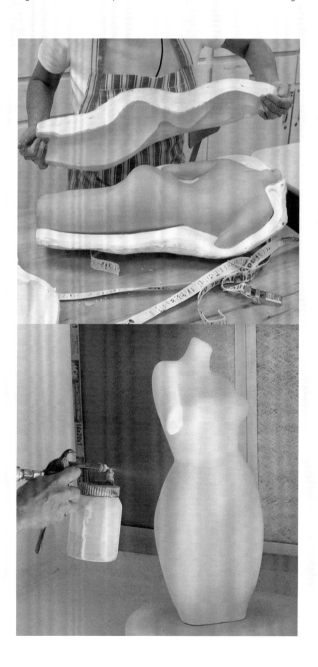

The low-down on china paints

China paint is essentially the lowest-firing form of glaze possible. It is almost always applied over a previously fired glaze and fired in oxidation to a temperature between Cones 019–014. China paint is usually supplied as a dry powder and mixed with a sticky medium for painting. Traditionally, the medium has been oil-based, usually some combination of turpentine (or its byproducts), the oils of lavender and clove, and a resin called balsam of copaiba. Today, china painters frequently turn to a water-soluble medium, usually glycerin, alcohol, sugar, or some form of gum or glycol.

Bridget Chérie Harper still has a supply of old colors from her initial purchase at the antique store, plus old paints given to her by friends. Since most ceramic suppliers do not carry china paints, she supplements these with colors imported from Dresden, Germany, by the Rynne China Company (www.rynnechina.com).

There are now china paints that are labeled "lead-free," but most china paints still contain lead, and, therefore, are not for surfaces that come into contact with food. However, several factors make them much less hazardous to use than lead glazes: The quantities used are tiny; there is no dust once the colors are mixed; and they do not volatilize in firing.

In contrast to painting with glazes or underglazes, china paint imagery is often built up slowly in successive firings. Often, decisions about color and texture are deferred until the painter sees the fired results of the last layer. The ability to wipe off and manipulate unfired paints opens a wide range of decorative possibilities.

For more information on china paint, including suppliers, books, teachers and an online discussion group, see Porcelain Painters International Online www.ppio.com.

Left: Bridget Chérie Harper china painting in her studio. Below: A few of Harper's vials of china paint, some of which are as much as one hundred years old.

Black on White
Modernizing Mimbres Decoration

by Tracy P. Gamble

PHOTOS BY DAVID L. GAMBLE

Mimbres–style vessel with contemporary silhouette of "Bob the Wonderdog," 8½ inches in height. Earthenware with white opaque matt glaze and single coat of gloss black decoration fired to cone 04.

The Mimbres people painted images in black on a white background, mostly on earthenware bowls. Very little beyond pottery has been recovered to learn more about these people, so making an interpretation of the Mimbres culture based on archaeological finds remains highly speculative. What is agreed upon, however, is that, between 550 and 1150 C.E., they lived in a 46-mile-long valley in a southwest corner of New Mexico. With no known incidence of war, these peaceful village dwellers also farmed, hunted and foraged. What is also agreed upon is that they painted on pottery, creating images of human figures with rabbits, lizards, fish, antelopes and even bugs from their landscape. It is interesting that Europe was rife with violence, war and religious imagery depicting agonies awaiting the damned in Hell during the same period that the Mimbres were painting images that appear to me to reflect a world viewed as an amiable cosmic circus.

I created a line of pottery celebrating the ancient art of the Mimbres people using their 900-year-old decorative motifs. These individually thrown and hand-painted, earthenware vessels are food, microwave and dishwasher safe for everyday appreciation of Mimbres artistry. The bowl form and antelope decoration of the vessels in the photographic examples was inspired directly from an authentic Mimbres piece in the Eiteljorg Museum collection in Indianapolis, Indiana. There are many images in traditional Mimbres decoration and some of those also appear on this line of pottery, such as the antelope, bird, lizard, fish and rabbit.

In my recent work, this Mimbres decorative style has progressed into more silhouette-type images from contemporary themes. For example, animal silhouettes—from dogs to chickens—as the main image on a vessel with Mimbres traditional rim designs are used. It's rewarding to celebrate ancient Mimbres artistry by making it new again on today's clay.

Using your template, trace the image onto the base glaze with a pencil.

Add the details, pencil marks will disappear during the kiln firing.

Using a small bamboo brush, paint the image with one coat of black, low-fire majolica glaze.

Center the vessel on the wheel or banding wheel and, as the vessel slowly turns, add 3 to 8 lines on and near the rim on the inside using a dagger brush.

Mark the centers of the small triangles that will go all the way around the rim.

Fill in triangles to complete the motif.

Research Mimbres designs on the internet by Googling "Mimbres designs." You'll find several sites with designs that will help you get started. You can also create contemporary designs in the Mimbres style. The antelope in the step-by-step photos on page 21, is a drawing based on original Mimbres imagery, which was photocopied to a size that best fit the vessel being glazed, then cut out with an X-Acto knife.

The Mimbres decoration is black on white. After bisque firing earthenware clay to cone 03, paint on three coats of an opaque white matt glaze for the white base/background. Apply the glaze one coat at a time and allow it to dry naturally between coats. Do not dry the coats with a hair dryer or heat gun since the heat shrinks the glaze quickly, causing it to separate from the clay and crawl during firing.

Use a soft lead pencil to trace a design on the white glaze base, then paint on the decoration using black glaze. If you use a gloss black, just a single coat will work if you want to keep the matt or satin effect of the white glaze. A second coat makes the black too glossy. Find a combination of clay and glazes you want to use and test them before investing a lot of time in decorating a piece. I've used various earthenware clay bodies and a variety of low-fire opaque matt white glazes and black glazes, all with good results.

Once the decoration was painted on, the vessel was final glaze fired to cone 04.

Mimbres–style antelope bowls ranging from 3 to 9 inches in diameter, wheel-thrown, red earthenware, fired to cone 04.

Mimbres–style lizard and rabbit vessels, wheel-thrown, earthenware, fired to cone 04, by Tracy Gamble.

No-Fire Decals

by Brendan Tang

"25 Years," ewer with Lazertran decal, flocking and wind-up key. Using nonfiring laser decals is an effective way to add printed elements to sculptural work.

Printing is an effective device in contemporary ceramic studio art, and offers the studio artist incomparable options for translating concepts through the application of imagery. Decals can be a cost- and time-effective approach to printing, and there are several types that can be used with ceramics. Regular commercial ceramic decals are fired at cone 017 and can withstand daily utilitarian use, mild abrasives, and exposure to direct sunlight without any degradation to the image. Because my works are nonfunctional and do not need to withstand a great deal of handling, I've produced and used color laser printed decals not normally intended for ceramic use. Laser printed decals are low cost in comparison to ceramic decals, which may include a large set-up fee. Heat-cured at low temperatures (within the range of a domestic oven), these decals are easy to use and permit economical experimentation and personalization. Laser printed decals do have limitations and drawbacks. They're for nonfunctional works only, as a bare decal can be easily scratched. Similarly, they do not have the same archival quality as decals produced specifically for ceramics.

Image preparation

Generally, my decals begin with digital photographs, often staged images of myself taken by an assistant. While photographic images suggest realistic portrayal, the images I use for decals are subject to manipula-

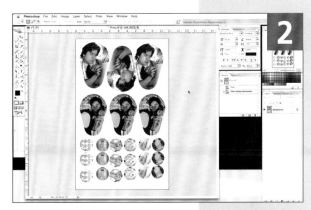

tion using computer graphics software (Adobe Photoshop). These self-portraits may be altered to exaggerate features, add elements or reconstruct the composition to greater inform the content of the work.

Begin with a digital image and, using Photoshop, alter the composition, color, shape, etc. (figure 1). The image that appears on the screen is a mirror image of what will appear on your piece. When you're finished working with the image, reverse it—this is especially important for text. When the images are complete, lay them out on a single page and include multiples. Having several copies of the same image helps you avoid additional trips to the printer (figure 2). Print the decals on Lazertran decal transfer paper on your printer (check compatibility at www.lazertran.com); or, have it printed at an office supply store. Either way, always print out a proof on plain paper first to check color.

Application

To apply the decals, you'll need a heat gun, scissors, squeegee (rubber rib), utility knife, cotton balls, rubbing alcohol, tray for water, decals and your ceramic work (figure 3). To ensure adherence and visibility, apply decals to clean, glazed white surfaces. The ceramic surface should be flat or gently curved so that the decal lies flat. Remove dirt, grease and oils by cleaning the surface with rubbing

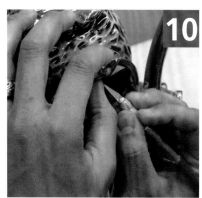

TIP

If you want a less glossy finish, omit the firing. If you do omit it, don't wipe the gum off the back of the decal and apply the decal to the piece face up (no mirror image needed). Apply a coat of clear polyacrylic paint to seal and protect the decal.

alcohol and a cotton ball (figure 4). Cut the decal to the desired size (figure 5). I use the proof page images as templates on awkwardly shaped forms to assist in correct sizing. Get a tight fit since any further trimming of the decal when it's in place may result in tearing.

To eliminate air bubbles trapped in the toner, use a heat gun to slowly and briefly heat the decal until it becomes shiny (figure 6). Be careful because overheating will damage the decal. Soak the decal in water until it releases the paper backing after it curls and relaxes (figure 7). Gently wipe the gum off the back of the decal with your fingers. If the gum is

not completely removed, it will turn brown when fired.

Place the decal on the surface, image-side down (figure 8). If necessary, apply heat from a hair dryer to help massage the decal over gentle curves. Use a rubber squeegee to remove any excess moisture or air bubbles from underneath the decal because air bubbles will rupture the surface of the decal when cured (figure 9). Also, make sure the edges are adhered to the ceramic surface, or they will curl and melt. Trim the decal with a craft knife, if necessary, but use caution to prevent tearing (figure 10).

"Out in the Cold," Lazertran and commercial decals, enamel paint.

"Royal with Cheese," Lazertran and commercial decals.

Firing

Before firing, the decal has a satin finish, which will become glossy once it is fired. Place the kiln/oven on the lowest possible temperature (approximately 150°F) and hold this temperature for at least an hour, then slowly raise the temperature every 20 minutes. The decal should become glossier as you approach 400°F. It's possible to get the desired glossy finish at a lower temperature (e.g., 290°F for "25 Years") if apply-

ing heat for a longer period of time. Check the piece every 15 minutes or so to see if you have gotten the desired finish. When done, shut off the heat and allow the piece to slowly cool in the oven or kiln. I sometimes rush the firing process or fail to remove all the air bubbles, which results in pinhole marks in the decal. If this happens to you, touch up the imperfections with acrylic paint, or you can remove decals with lacquer thinner if necessary.

Darren Emenau
Lichen Surfaces

by Mandy Ginson

Detail of a covered jar made from local cone 06 earthenware with MNO Lichen Glaze.

Texture takes on an important role in Emenau's recent work. Impurities, such as twigs and stones, are not removed but rather retained to effect unique markings and interesting surfaces. The roughed-up, worn exteriors convey a rich sense of history. This is not by chance. Individual works have been fired up to eight or nine times. History is not imitated but created. Emenau is a self-professed glaze fanatic. As he increasingly exploits this knowledge, the glaze is used not as mere surface decoration but the surface itself. Emenau experiments with applying successive layers of glaze and refiring. The results, he admits, might be irreproducible, but the intent here is not to make models but rather to unearth possibilities.

The thick crusts, pocked surfaces and acidic earthy colors in "Lichen," the most recent body of work to exit the studio, closely resemble the natural formations they are inspired by.

The jugs, bud vases and bowls, in their simple but solid shape, team a roughed-up classical form with a rugged organic minimalism. In the Lichen series, a certain sense of layered narrative is staged, with one eye cocked to the prankish. Emenau continues to create opportunities for discovery in his work. Currently he is experimenting with glazes developed from indigenous rocks. Quartz, limestone and granite are crushed with mortar and pestle, then further refined with the aide of a sieve.

Emenau's work is simple in the smartest of ways. In breaking the universe down to its smallest bits and coming to understand the nature, identity and composition of each of these bits, Emenau is able to make sense of a complex world. His work continues to stir the imagination and supplies viewers with a renewed opportunity to fully experience the natural world and all of its inherent wonders.

Above: Sake Set, to 4½ inches in height.

Below: Tea Set, to 6 inches in height. Both are local earthenware, fired to cone 06.

Recipe

MNO Lichen
Cone 06

Borax	24.7%
Lithium Carbonate	9.3
Magnesium Carbonate	39.2
Ferro Frit 3134	3.1
Nepheline Syenite	23.7
	100.0%
Add: Copper Carbonate	5.2%
Bentonite	3.1%

This recipe was inspired by low-fire recipes by Lana Wilson. I brush it on in various thicknesses. Some of the glaze can flake off during firings. After firing, I scrape or sand blast the surface to remove any loose glaze. I rub beeswax into some areas and then torch it to remove most of the wax. Forms are often multifired. A nepheline syenite wash prevents flaking during firings. My local clay contains a high percentage of iron oxide and salt crystals, which act as strong fluxes.

"Bud Vase," 5 inches in height, local earthenware, with MNO Lichen Glaze, fired to cone 06.

"Ellie Euer," 4 inches in height, local earthenware, with MNO Lichen Glaze, fired to cone 06.

Lee Akins
Intricate Surfaces

by Rafael Molina-Rodriguez

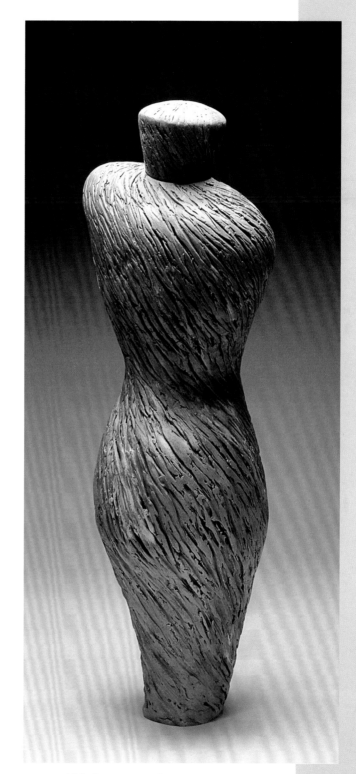

**"Torso Lidded Jar," 20 inches in
height, coil-built terra cotta, with
Peeling Paint Glaze, fired to cone 01
in oxidation, motivated by a wall and
boards seen in the Philippines.**

Dallas, Texas, ceramist and educator Lee Akins' work in clay is ostensibly sculptural in nature, but upon closer inspection it reveals its vessel structure. The forms reference the human figure; the surfaces are inspired by natural and man-made objects.

The surfaces of Akins' work are very intricate. The texture, pattern, color and value are the result of tool marks, ceramic media, and firing processes. "Earthenware clay," says Akins, "gives warmth to the colors, yet allows a wide choice of finishes." The texture is derived from Akins' conscious effort to leave marks of the forming process, rather than covering them up. Additionally, some marks are from stamps (found and made) and others are from textured paddles.

Color in Akins' work is the product of stains and glazes as well as the firing atmosphere. One of his favorite colorants to work with is copper carbonate. "Painting copper on and wiping it away is one of my favorite techniques. It's very simple, yet very effective. Earthenware seems to

A piece of weathered wood from Lake Katherine in New Mexico is just one of many natural surfaces that inspire Akins' work.

take on a sheen with copper," Akins explains.

To develop a patina, Akins uses commercial underglazes layered with oxides. They give a strong, intense color and bring out the texture. In oxidation firing he glazes and layers more. He elaborates, "It's more like painting on a piece. Many times I'll build up by putting a material on and sanding it off. I'll then apply another one and dust it off. Finally, I'll apply another one unevenly."

Traditionally, earthenware is fired to cone 04 (1971°F). The temperature range at which Akins' work is fired is cone 01 (2080°F) to cone 1 (2109°F). "Firing higher affects the color. It also affects the clay. It's harder and more vitrified. When struck it has a nice ring to it," he says. During his career, Akins has fired his work in oxidizing and reducing atmospheres. Most of his recent work is fired in an electric kiln; however, a few pieces are fired in a fuel-burning kiln.

Recipes

Scotchie Crackle Slip
Cones 04–01
Gerstley Borate	25 %
Kaolin	50
Silica	25
	100 %

Use on leather-hard clay.

Piepenburg Patina
Cones 04–01
Bone Ash	33 %
Gerstley Borate	45
Nepheline Syenite	22
	100 %

Textured Ash Engobe
Cones 04–7
Alumina Hydrate	20 %
Gerstley Borate	10
Unwashed Wood Ash	50
Kaolin	20
	100 %
Add: Fine Grog	15 %

Messenger Crawl
Cones 06–01
Borax	4 %
Gerstley Borate	46
Magnesium Carbonate	31
Kaolin	19
	100 %
Add: Zircopax	5 %

Lichen Glaze
Cones 06–01
Gerstley Borate	50 %
Magnesium Carbonate	50
	100 %

Peeling Paint
Cones 08–01
Gerstley Borate	80 %
Titanium Dioxide	20
	100 %

For Green
Add: Copper Carbonate	3–5%

For Blue
Add: Cobalt Carbonate	3 %

For Black
Add: Cobalt Carbonate	5 %
Red Iron Oxide	5 %
Black Stain	10 %

"Round Jar," 17 inches in height, coil-built terra cotta, with copper oxide, fired in oxidation, inspired by a red wall in Portland, Oregon.

"Green Jar," 19 inches in height, coil-built terra cotta, with Scotchie Crackle Slip and copper oxide, fired to cone 01 in oxidation. The surface of this piece was inspired by a cave wall in Gunung Kawai, Indonesia, shown above.

Tea and Friskets

by Frank James Fisher

"Sunoco Tea-Can," 6¼ inches in height, thrown and hand-built porcelain, raku fired, with metal and wood handle. All of my work is rooted in the commercial world. Marketing is everywhere we look. It is part of life. I embrace the impact of advertising and use it frequently. Applying a logo and graphics changes a ceramic piece from a generic sculpture into a singular American object. The use of logos and brands is a shortcut to the viewer. It provides instant common ground for artist and audience. It gives the work immediate, real-world, daily-life context.

For the last few years I've been creating teapots that I refer to as "Tea-Cans." They owe a great deal to industrial fuel-can designs and all the various plumbing fixtures found around the workshop. The glaze effects on these tea-cans slowly evolved over four years with the first tests starting at cone 10 reduction firing and finally ending at cone 06 raku firing.

There are many ways to reproduce a graphic image on ceramic surfaces—decals, transfers, screen-printing or even applying paints. The guiding force behind each technique is to control and present a precise image on the ceramic surface. I wanted a method of reproducing the look of a printed graphic—something where the graphics would not only be a part of the overall glazed surface, but actually be the glazed surface. Using a range of glazes, my experience in painting, airbrushing and commercial printing, along with a few new twists to control the glaze application, creating a graphic from glazes evolved.

Finding a way to enliven the predictable but plastic-looking glaze color required something in between

Spectrum glazes (other commercial glazes would work as well) provide the intense commercial paint colors found in mass-produced products and printed logos. My own hand-mixed raku glazes offset the intense commercial hues. I like the balance achieved by incorporating both types of glaze mixes: intense commercial color versus the more unpredictable earth tones.

Use an image as-is or manipulate them using image software and print several copies.

Cut through two sheets of paper at the same time so you'll have a second set for a back up.

Label each frisket, then check for color and fit.

Spray adhesive on the back of the frisket.

two extremes. I wanted controlled glaze edges, but with vibrant areas of color. My application method provided accuracy, but the "lively color" owes as much to the raku process as to my glazes or glazing techniques. Raku firing provides an aged and worn color palette to the tea-can not achievable in other firing methods, and also lends a touch of spontaneity into my art. Here is the technique I developed and use with a reasonable

degree of success. The tea-can in the photos is bisque-fired porcelain.

Process

Find an image. Applying a real-world logo to my forms adds a stronger impact to my work. The Internet, especially eBay, is a great source for industrial shapes and graphics. After locating a 50-year-old oilcan logo (figure 1), I stretched and pulled the digital image until it was the perfect size and shape.

Use a Post-It note to hold small pieces while spraying.

Sponge the glaze within the masked bare clay surface.

Carefully remove the frisket when glaze is dry.

Attach the next frisket and apply glaze.

A frisket is used in airbrushing to mask off areas you do not want to spray. To make a frisket, take the printout and carefully cut out the printed shapes and letters with a sharp knife (figure 2). For each color, you'll need a different frisket. Label each frisket with the color and the order it is to be applied (figure 3). Make sure to double check your work for fit. Note: Determining the order in which the friskets are applied is a key element of the design, and the first one is often the most complicated one you've cut.

The paper frisket needs to adhere to the bisqued surface. Set up a quick spray booth with a cardboard box and hold the frisket with its reverse side toward you. Using spray mount adhesive (I prefer 3M Spray Mount Artist's Adhesive), evenly coat the frisket. Keep the booth set up and spray each frisket as needed.

Two glaze colors have been applied and friskets removed.

Apply base color and trim glazes after applying detailed design work.

Use an old toothbrush to speckle the glaze surface.

Applying and allowing the edges of two glazes to touch may result in blurred or melted edges. Control the integrity of the edge by leaving a thin line of bare bisque surface between the colors to prevent bleeding. For my work, I prefer the colors to blend as it provides a nice balance to the tight execution of the logo image.

Caution: Protect your hands with disposable rubber gloves (figures 4).

The entire design keys off the first frisket, which will help you position successive colors, so mentally plan the process once more to be sure of placement. You may want to practice the technique on a piece of paper first before attempting it on your bisqued piece. When the adhesive is dry but tacky, position and press the frisket into place. Dab a stamping sponge into the glaze and apply the color (figure 5). When the glaze has fully dried to a chalky texture on the frisket, it's safe to peel away (figure 6). Peeling the frisket while the glaze is still damp results in tearing, leaving adhesive residue stuck on the bisqued surface.

Repeat the previous step for each color and for each frisket you've made (figure 7). If the frisket touches already glazed areas, the glue will not stick to the chalky surface. In these cases, tape a frisket without the spray adhesive firmly in place and sponge the glaze onto

the surface. Since there is no glue, you may remove the frisket immediately (figure 8).

Note: I always glaze the logo first because of all the jostling during the application of the many little design elements. If I glazed the larger but simpler areas first, those surfaces could be rubbed off and ruined while glazing the logo.

Use a frisket to protect the finished logo while applying glaze next to the logo's edge. This design has two large areas of color so I taped off the bottom rim for a second accent color. Apply each color in turn (figure 9). The final result is a precisely glazed logo and a tea-can ready for firing . . . almost.

Since everything is too clean and precise, I like to add a little chaos to the surface. After setting up another quick spray booth and placing the tea-can into position, I glaze the lid, which doesn't have any tight color areas, only an aged metal look. Now it's time to splatter, drip, fling, smear and wipe the glaze across the surface. Use a stiff toothbrush and assorted hobby brushes to launch the glaze in an even-handed but haphazard manner at the surface (figure 10). Some glazed areas are dry wiped with a stiff paper towel to thin the glaze application. Other areas are wiped damp or even scratched to reveal a bare bisque surface that will become blackened during the postfiring reduction. The tea-can is now ready to raku fire (figure 11).

Applying glazes with sponges reduces the need for overspray masking needed when airbrushing. Sponging contributes to a healthier studio environment as well; however, airbrushing is still an excellent technique to produce glaze color gradations.

Carol Gouthro
Mastering the Surface

by Judy Wagonfeld

Architect Robert Venturi once remarked, "Less is a bore." Ceramist Carol Gouthro, like Venturi, advocates design exuberance and embellishment. Her glitzy biomorphic vessels and goblets read Baroque meets sci-fi, the antithesis of Bauhaus simplicity. To Gouthro's way of thinking, minimalism negates the complexity of contemporary life. Rather than striving to escape the fray, she embraces its diversity and craziness.

As if a wacky horticulturist, Gouthro seeks mutant hybrids. Borrowing from botanical forms and mundane household objects, she throws, slab builds and casts forms that merge and metamorphose into quirky sculptures. The foot-high works blaze with sumptuous glazes, slips, terra sigillatas and underglazes. Shrunk to half the size of her earlier sleeker vases, these enigmatic shape-shifters venture into a less realistic, edgy realm. Accentuated by Gouthro's hallmark kaleidoscopic hues, they glow like rainbows after a storm, exuding visceral joy. Preening as voguish envoys from an exotic paradise, they handily dismiss doom.

Gouthro, a master of unique finishes, constantly dreams up dazzling brocades of color. Recorded in a six-inch-thick recipe book, they refresh her memory, a necessary step when making many of her own glazes and array of smooth, crusty tactile surfaces and luminous lusters. Captivated by these unusual qualities, viewers want to fondle the maze-hued spiny points punctuating the salmon colored cup of "Floris #2."

In most pieces, the top section vaguely resembles a flower. These petaled orifices and phallic-filled

**"Floris #1 and #2,"
12 inches in height,
slip-cast and hand-
built terra cotta and
white earthenware
with slips, stains,
underglazes, glazes
and lusters, fired to
cone 04.**

interiors, fired in luscious and glossy glazes, recall the eroticism of Judy Chicago's "Dinner Party" plates, the paintings of Georgia O'Keefe and the goofiness of Funk Art. Although this anthropomorphic femininity forms a component of sexuality in Gouthro's vessels, it also alludes to a broad swath of women's multi-tasked lives.

For Gouthro, who teaches, makes and sells production-based tableware and spends spare moments nurturing a prolific garden, the component parts reflect her balancing act of time, finances and domestic responsibilities. Art and life meld in daily thoughts. Nostalgia plays an important role. A Jell-o mold, cast in plaster and sliced into varying parts, becomes a base. A rubber dog toy, enhanced through wax erosion and cut into bony segments, mimics a spine. Metal bees, cast into clay, emerge from a sea-green vessel glaze.

Inspired by nature's botanical shapes found in gardens and wild lands, Gouthro delves into research for her projects. Studying historical floral illustrations and photography, she's been inspired by the close-up plant microphotography of German photographer Karl Blossfeldt (1865–1932). Focusing on the menacing qualities of spikes, holes and insect-like legs, she merges them with benign fairy tale swans, ducklings and frogs, building outlandish organic structures.

Gouthro fearlessly mixes traditional black-and-white stripes, vines and leaves juxtaposed with Pop Art papaya, turquoise and chartreuse hues. Meshing all into a cogent whole looks back to pattern-and-decoration artist Miriam Schapiro, as well as Mexican folk art. Floral concepts, as if viewed while on a mind-altering drug, burgeon as in Yves Tanguy's surrealist aberrations of nature's elements. In "Floris #1", a Creamsicle-hued vertebral stem grows from chartreuse leaves. At the top, a perky orange stamen rises from the interior of its dusky blue flower.

Gouthro's signature use of glistening "raised droplets" of beaded glaze, when dry, resembles morning dew. Spiky globules, applied by slip-trailed drops, impart the danger of nature's protective thorns. Dull sheen finishes, achieved through a wax erosion stage followed by sponge rubbing produces a soft, eroded-over-time appearance. Repeated color layers, sanded with steel wool, evolve to eerie mottling. Multiple firings of natural terra cotta clay yield stunning coppery hues.

Gouthro's voluptuous segments, combined in vertical stacks, reflect Asian temples, ornately carved statuary and over-the-top Venetian glass. Her obsessive attention to detail and repeated glaze firings allow each work's personality to blossom. Through bumps, quills and pitting, she contrasts rough and smooth, and the sponge and lichen textures that echo nature. To create pock marks, holes and lines, Gouthro carves leather-hard clay with a dental tool, pokes it with a wire brush and molds around the bumpy outsides of golf balls. Painstakingly piercing the clay shapes with a hollow metal tube transforms a goblet bowl into a hole-punched, lotus pod, botanical colander.

Unswervingly, Gouthro's theatrical, lush work projects a primeval voice. Never a shrinking violet, it bursts forth with the splendor of a mountain meadow, juxtaposing serenity and commotion. Free of decay, each mutant, as if a futuristic artifact, seduces like erotic eye candy. Though the bricolage towers hint at danger, a celebratory fiesta of sexuality and hope prevails. Each flamboyant piece reminds us to seek beauty and possibility while navigating the riotous garden of modern life.

"Floris #6," 24 inches in height, thrown and handbuilt earthenware with slips, stains and glazes, fired to cone 04, by Carol Gouthro, Seattle, Washington.

The Ceramic Surface

by Carol Gouthro

The smaller, intimate scale of the "Floris" series allows me to focus on detail and indulge my love of embellishment, sensuous surfaces, rich, intense color, intricate pattern and texture. The ceramic glaze process is one that I enjoy immensely and I spend hours painting and firing every piece, often four and five times.

"Floris #4" demonstrates several surface design techniques:

Beaded Glaze: By beading glaze up on the bisque surface, I form sparkling droplets, evocative of dew. After glaze firing, I use a magnifying glass and tiny brush to luster each drop. Though this requires hours, the dazzling effect makes the time well spent.

Wax Resist: To achieve my black and white patterns I favor wax-resist techniques. First, I paint white underglaze on bone-dry surfaces. After that dries, I paint patterns with wax resist. This preserves the white areas when I cover the entire surface with a black underglaze. I've found that wax resist is the surest method to fabricate an intricate pattern with crisp, sharp edges.

Raised Patterns: To make the raised thorn pattern on the small spherical forms, I squeeze thick, colored slip through a fine tipped hair-dye applicator bottle. After tinting the slips with colorants and Mason stains, I cover the surfaces with a colored transparent glaze. The resulting sharp tactile surface is reminiscent of forms in nature.

"Floris #4," 11½ inches in height, slip-cast and handbuilt earthenware with slip trailing, wax-resist, underglaze, glazes and lusters, fired to cone 04.

Mary Barringer
Conversing with the Surface

by Leigh Taylor Mickelson

Within Mary Barringer's work, there is a balance, or rather a tension, between form and function, texture and line, color and image, hard and soft, warm and cool. Although fired to cone 6 in an electric kiln, the surfaces have a richness and depth that I had thought could only be achieved in a reduction atmosphere.

Barringer creates a texture—lines, scratches, punctures, grooves—with her many tools. Then she brushes on some slip, scrapes it off, brushes on another slip, wipes it off with a green scrub pad, over and over. And once the pot has been bisque fired, she begins again, layering on various thicknesses of slips and glazes, then scraping or wiping them off.

Here, especially, her technique mirrors the weathering of the New England landscape—the rhythmic motions and fortuitous scraping of making and erasing marks.

These marks are an essential part of the conversation that her pots have with their viewers.

Barringer incorporates a red dot into a number of her pieces—plates, creamers, dishes and basins—drawing the eye out of the thick layers of slip and texture to this poignant, potent splash of color. The red gives us something to focus on—a spot of color within the rich earth tones, a familiar place to see and touch as you hold the piece, rotating it in your hands. It speaks of the kind of familiarity that relates comfort, like your

Left: Rectangular platter, 13 inches in length, slab-built and incised stoneware, with multiple slips, fired to cone 6.

Right: Rectangular platter, 14 inches in length, slab-built and incised stoneware, with multiple slips, fired to cone 6.

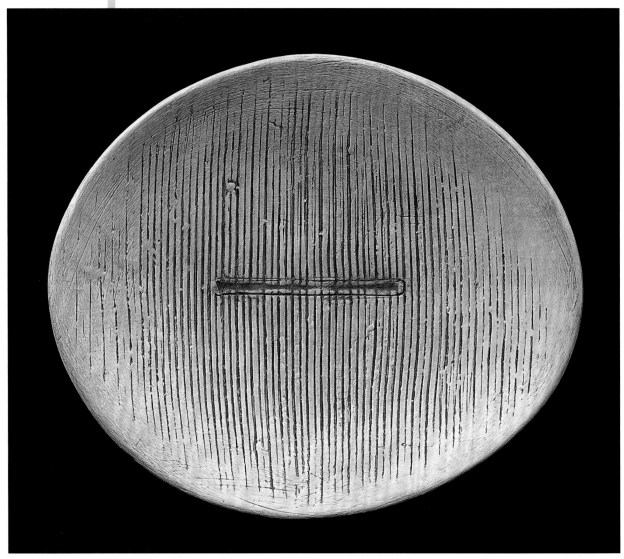

Ovoid dish, 12 inches in length, slab-built and incised stoneware, with multiple slips, fired to cone 6.

favorite coffee mug in the morning or those hand-knit wool socks that you wear on cold days.

There is no doubt that Barringer is "fascinated by the conversation that goes on between people and things—and between people through things—and I want to participate in that with my work. It means engag-

ing in ideas that are not just personal, and that my personal exploration goes on against the backdrop of a larger, cultural set of ideas about objects and functions. I like that my pots go out and lead a life separate from me, and become a part of someone else's life. That potential is a huge gift for a potter."

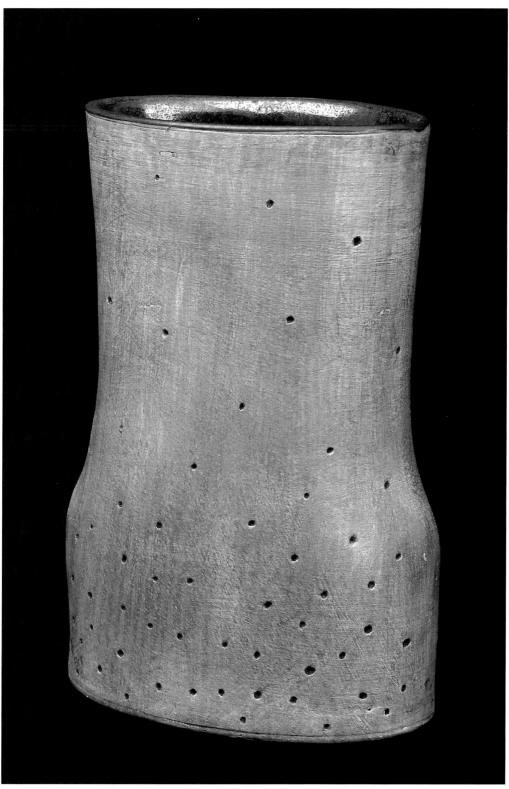

Vase, 9 inches in height, stoneware, with multiple slips, fired to cone 6.

Creamer, 4¼ inches in height, slab-built stoneware, with multiple slips, fired to cone 6.

Teapot, 6½ inches in height, handbuilt stoneware, with slip, fired to cone 6, by Mary Barringer.

Recipes

White Slip Base
Cone 6

Ferro Frit 3124	10 %
Nepheline Syenite	15
Ball Clay	25
EPK Kaolin	25
Silica	25
	100%

Color variations are mixed with the following additions.

Black
Black Stain	10 %
Red Iron Oxide	8 %

Blue-Black
Black Stain	10%
Cobalt Carbonate	2 %

Gray-Green
Chrome Oxide	3 %
Copper Carbonate	3 %

Light Green
Copper Carbonate	5 %

Strong Green
Chrome Oxide	6 %

Blue-Green
Chrome Oxide	3%
Cobalt Carbonate	1.5%

Teal
Copper Carbonate	3 %
Teal Stain	6 %

Medium Blue
Cobalt Carbonate	1 %
Rutile	3 %

Cream
Rutile	5 %

Yellow
Yellow Stain	10 %

Pink
Pink Stain	10 %

Recipes

Vitreous Black Slip

Cone 6

Borax	10 %
Nepheline Syenite	23
Kaolin	22
Ball Clay	23
Silica	22
	100%
Add: Cobalt Oxide	1.0%
Copper Oxide	4.5%
Red Iron Oxide	4.5%

Redart Slip

Cone 6

Lithium Carbonate	10 %
Spodumene	10
Cedar Heights Redart	80
	100 %
Add: Red Iron Oxide	2 %

Ash Engobe

Cone 6

Talc	15 %
Wood Ash (unwashed)	20
Cornwall Stone	25
Ferro Frit 3124	15
Ball Clay	25
	100 %

For white/tan variation, add 7.5% tin ox.; for pink/
brown, add 1.5% nickel oxide and 8% pink stain.

Chinese Ash Slip

Cone 6

Wood Ash	50 %
Ball Clay	50
	100 %
Add: Gerstley Borate	3 %

Single-Fire Ash Glaze

Cone 6

Wood Ash	19 %
Potash Feldspar	25
Kaolin	12
Red Clay	13
Silica	31
	100 %
Add: Cobalt Carbonate	1–5 %
Red Iron Oxide	15 %

Burlington Base Glaze

Cone 6

Lithium Carbonate	2.0%
Strontium Carbonate	5.4
Whiting	12.2
Soda Feldspar	20.4
Albany Slip	22.4
Ball Clay	25.4
Zircopax	12.2
	100.0%

Color variations are possible with oxide, carbonate
and/or stain additions.

RC Slip

Cone 6

Whiting	30 %
Kona F-4 Feldspar	20
Cedar Heights Redart	40
Silica	10
	100 %

Sheen-O Glaze

Cone 6

Soda Ash	2.9%
Gerstley Borate	4.9
Spodumene	22.8
Nepheline Syenite	54.5
Ball Clay	14.9
	100.0%
Add: Chrome	0.5%

Glassy Slip

Cone 6

Gerstley Borate	5 %
Lithium Carbonate	80
Bentonite	15
	100 %

Dense White Engobe

Cone 6

Ferro Frit 3110	10 %
Nepheline Syenite	20
Ball Clay	30
Zircopax	40
	100 %
Add: Bentonite	2 %
Macaloid	1 %

Yellow Oxide Glaze

Cone 6

Lithium Carbonate	4.5%
Zinc Oxide	18.5
Ferro Frit 3110	28.0
Kaolin	31.5
Silica	17.5
	100.0%
Add: Tin Oxide	4.5%
Copper Carbonate	0.5%
Iron Oxide	4.5%
Yellow Ocher	0.5%

Metallic Black Glaze

Cone 6

Gerstley Borate	11 %
Whiting	5
Feldspar	79
Kaolin	5
	100 %
Add: Cobalt Oxide	2 %
Copper Carbonate	4 %
Manganese Dioxide	4 %

Super-Dry Matt Glaze

Cone 6

Gerstley Borate	5 %
Lithium Carbonate	6
Strontium Carbonate	15
Nepheline Syenite	60
Calcined Clay	8
Silica	6
	100 %

Color variations are possible with oxide, carbonate
and/or stain additions.

Stevenson Vitreous Engobe

Cone 6

Whiting	3 %
Feldspar	8
Ferro Frit 3124	45
Ball Clay	10
Kaolin	12
Silica	12
Tin Oxide	10
	100 %

Fusing Clay and Dichroic Glass

by Alfred Spivack

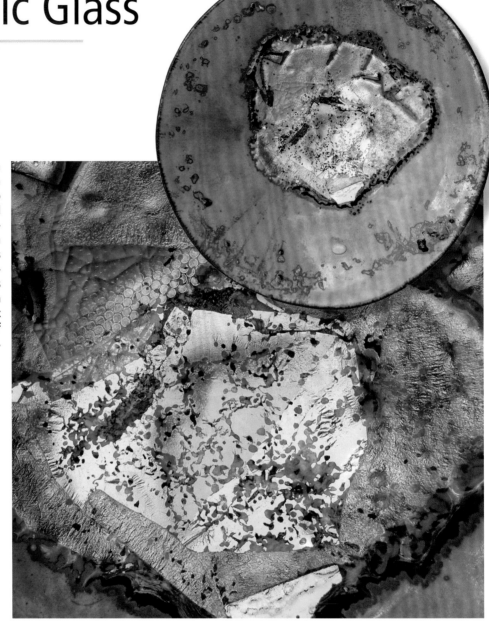

Platter, 15 inches in diameter, thrown stoneware fired to cone 6 then refired with glass following the program outlined. The glass is composed of multiple colors of glass frits and random pieces of dichroic glass. Left: detail of glass area.

As a youth, I was fascinated by the way light produced a rainbow of colors in kaleidoscopes and when passing through the optical prism. To me the finding and unlocking of colors is magic. It was no surprise that my first exposure to dichroic glass art works drew me in to view them at multiple angles and experience the color changes.

As I looked at squares of clear-backed dichroic glass directly, I saw brilliant reflections of light, and as the glass was rotated I could see the translucency, transparency and color changes. My response to the beauty of the glass was to consider the possibilities of adding it to ceramics. The reality check came when I asked experts in both ceramics and glass about combining the dichroic glass with clay. The answer was that it wouldn't work because there are too many variables in the expansion and contraction of differing media. I was also warned that dichroic glass would burn off at clay firing temperatures. Looking back on my years as a cardiologist, however, it occurred to me that I had heard that futility message before and realized that some of the successes in my medical career came from taking the road not taken.

Dichroic glass is glass coated with a thin film of metallic oxides, such as titanium and combinations of other metals, which have been vaporized by an electronic beam. The coatings allow certain wavelengths to be reflected and others to be transmitted. The term dichroic relates to having multiple colors. The technology came from the space industry and subsequently found its way into glass art. For its use in ceramics, I visualized glaze painting on ceramic surfaces and fusing the glass over the images in order to create a window of varying images. Once the process was made to work, combinations of sheet glass and dichroic glass could be used. With the use of a ring glass cutter (I use the Taurus 3, which can be found at www.geminisaw.com), the shapes and forms that can be created are endless. I hoped to entice the viewer into walking around the art work in order to view the changing visual effects of the glass-surfaced clay. The only detail to be worked out was how to make the fu-

sion work and preserve the surface and shape of the glass. After all, it is not a problem to melt glass into liquid form and make it stick.

Finding a low-fire program to use for glass fusing on the already-glazed and fired ceramics was the challenge. My plan to attempt fusion was to start at the extremes of high and low temperatures and work toward a satisfactory program. Knowing that glass slumps at 1300°F and is liquid at the temperatures of clay vitrification, I determined to first bisque and then glaze and fire the ceramics. Starting with Cone 06 as the highest temperature and working downward, a satisfactory program evolved after many firings. It appears that staying below 1500°F preserves the shape and surface of the dichroic and thin sheet art glass. Firing at higher temperatures is more likely to burn off the dichroic surface layer and create bubbles.

A few companies manufacture art and dichroic glass. I have chosen to use Bullseye thin glass (www.bullseyeglass.com) in both the dichroic and colored sheet glass. Compatibility of glasses in multilayered glass fusion is important and necessary for optimal fusion.

At first I used single squares of dichroic glass applied to the ceramics with commercial GlasTac, a glue used in glass kiln forming that holds pieces in place prior to firing. The previously glazed and fired ceramics were fired again at the lower temperatures. As I became more confident with the process, I used

Firing for Fusion

The program that follows should be viewed as a starting point. Each kiln has its own properties and, depending on the complexity and size of the glass pieces used, the slumping, annealing and fusion times may need to be adjusted. Having a kiln with a computer allows the stages of the program to be preset on the ramp-hold portion of the kiln computer. The highest temperature that I currently use is 1450°F with a hold period of 15–30 minutes. This level preserves the shapes and surfaces of the glasses and allows the layers of glass to fuse to the clay surface and to each other and lessens the problem of bubble formation. I currently do the annealing of the glass during the cooling phase at 950°F and hold for 30–45 minutes. CAUTION: Do not open the kiln for a peek. I wait a day after the firing is finished and let the kiln cool to room temperature.

I currently use a five-segment ramp-hold program, which is set on the computer control of my kiln:

Segment 1: 150°/hour to 750°F

Segment 2: 200°/hour to 1150°F

Segment 3: 250°/hour to 1450°F, hold 15–30 minutes

Segment 4: 300°/hour to 950°F, hold 30–45 minutes

Segment 5: 300°/hour to 150°F

Then let the kiln cool until the contents are at room temperature.

Detail of thrown stoneware platter with bronze glaze, fired to cone 8, then refired with glass following the program provided above. Three layers of glass were simultaneously fired to create this effect.

multiple layers of glass and began to cut forms and designs. With dichroic glass, the coating is only on one surface. In order to determine top and bottom, hold the glass to light and look at the edge. On the top, the film extends to the edge, while the undersurface shows a clear edge from the thickness of the glass.

I have found that the larger the individual piece of glass and the more heat that is applied (determined by both temperature and duration of heat) the more likely the result will show bubbles in the glass. The bubbles are probably the result of thin spots created in the glass from excess heat and trapping of air when the glass cools. Initially I used low-fire glazes on the clay, thinking that the lower-firing glazes would help with better fusion, I now use a variety of low- and high-fire glazes and have even fused glass to unglazed clay. If I am not satisfied with the resultant design or bubbles have occurred, I refire with additional glass, glass frit or a combination. In the five years in which I have been fusing glass to clay, I have not had glass pop off, which is what I was told would happen.

Once the techniques of fusion are shown to be reliable, there are endless possibilities of composition. Using a ring cutter makes it remarkably easy to cut complex forms of glass and, if used properly, seems to have a good degree of safety. The possibilities then are those of the skill and imagination of the artist.